The Great
MECHANICAL
WOODEN TOY
Book

The Great MECHANICAL WOODEN TOY Book

A Family Workshop Book
By Ed & Stevie Baldwin

Chilton Book Company
Radnor, Pennsylvania

Copyright 1984 by The Family Workshop
Published in Radnor, Pa. by Chilton Book Company
Library of Congress Catalog Card Number: 84-45354
ISBN: 0-8019-7508-5
Manufactured in the United States of America

Created by The Family Workshop, Inc.
Editorial Director: Janet Weberling
Editors: Mike McUsic, Rhonda Mulberry, Mary Milander, Suzi West
Art Director: Dale Crain
Technical Artist: Roberta Taff
Production Artists: Wanda Young, Janice Harris Burstall, Verna Stonecipher-Fuller
Typography: Deborah Gahm
Creative Director: April Bail
Workshop Director: D.J. Olin
Photography: Bill Welch
Project Designs: Ed and Stevie Baldwin, D.J. Olin, April Bail, Roberta Taff

1 2 3 4 5 6 7 8 9 0   3 2 1 0 9 8 7 6 5 4

This book is dedicated to Andrea, who didn't mind the long hours, and to Matthew, who didn't mind playing with the toys.

Preface

Toys are for having fun. The mechanical wooden toys featured in this book are fun not only for the kids who get to play with them, but for the grown-ups who create them. We delighted in designing our favorite wooden toys, and figuring out how to make them go. The innards of some of these contraptions may look like spaghetti at first, but the component parts are not difficult to fashion.

The book begins with a section on tips and techniques for buying and working with wood. We strongly recommend that you read this section before beginning any of the projects. It provides basic information on materials, tools, and terminology for the beginner, and might just teach an old pro a new trick.

Each project plan contains a list of materials and provides thoroughly illustrated step-by-step instructions for building and finishing that particular wooden toy. Almost all projects can be built using common hand tools or hand-held power tools.

We would like to offer special thanks to a number of companies who provided some of the materials, tools, or services for building the projects. Tools supplied by Black & Decker, Shopsmith, and Singer performed superbly. The stain, which produced such a fine finish on some of the projects, was provided by Watco-Dennis Corporation. Last, but not least, we would like to thank the Frank Paxton Lumber Company for providing lumber.

We hope you'll find, as we did, that all the cranks and gears and pulleys and itty-bitty pieces will wind up as toys that delight and amuse your high-tech children — and bring them a taste of life before computer chip toys.

Contents

Tips & Techniques

Every toymaker since Geppetto (you remember Pinocchio) has his or her own tried-and-true techniques for shaping wood into a finished toy. These suggestions are not an attempt to persuade you away from the way you do things best, but are intended to provide some essential information concerning the materials, terms, and techniques that we used for the projects in this book. Some of the information may be old hat to you – some may be new – and some you may disagree with. If there's one thing we know for certain about toymakers, it's that we all approach the art of woodworking a bit differently.

Included here you'll find discussions of various types of lumber, finishes, adhesives, fasteners, joints, and some miscellanea that will be helpful in using this book. We suggest that you read this section all the way through, or at least scan it, before you begin work on any project.

WOODWORKING TIPS

Selecting Wood

Different types of wood often have vastly different characteristics. This makes certain woods better for specific purposes than others. In addition, lumber is graded according to quality. We'll talk about types of wood first, then we'll discuss the grading system.

Woods are divided into two general categories: hard and soft. Most hardwoods are much more difficult to cut and work with, but usually are more sturdy and long-lived than softwoods. Softwoods are a lot easier to work with. The most commonly available softwoods are fir, redwood, hemlock, cedar, cypress, larch, spruce, and pine. Douglas is a particularly good fir; pine usually is available in both white (finer grain) and yellow (coarser grain).

Softwoods vary widely in their tendency to shrink, swell, and warp. Those least likely to do so are redwood, white pine, spruce, cedar, and cypress. Part of what determines the quality of a board is the portion of the tree from which it is cut. **Figure A** illustrates the difference between a heartwood board and one that is cut farther from the center of the tree. The more densely-packed annual rings near the center of the tree produce a higher-quality board, while boards cut from farther out may absorb moisture and warp, rendering a tricky toy mechanism sticky and about as much fun as trying to open Grandma's windows after a spring rain. At the lumberyard, examine the ends of the boards carefully. The pattern of and distance between rings will tell you a lot about how long your children's mechanical wooden toys will last.

Lumber is graded, as we mentioned earlier. We have provided a rundown of the grading system for pine, which is also used for most other types of lumber. Keep firmly in mind that you need not use the highest grade of lumber for every (or any) project. If you are in doubt as to which grade to use for a specific project, talk it over with your lumber dealer. Show him the plans so he gets the whole picture.

#5 common – Full of knots, knotholes, and other headaches but the least expensive, this grade of lumber should be used only when structural strength is not re-

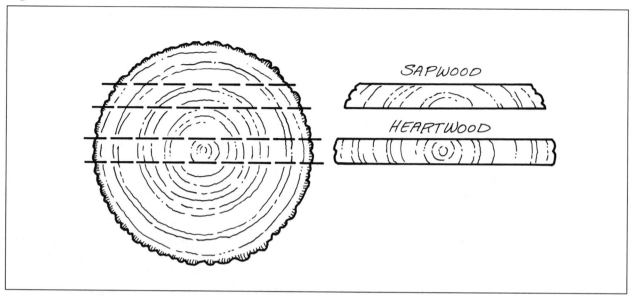

quired and when you intend to paint. It is prone to check (crack along the grain), and usually will not be as thoroughly seasoned or dried as the higher grades.

#4 common – This grade is low in cost and has lots of imperfections, but less so than #5. It is good for projects in which appearance is not crucial.

#3 common – Small knotholes are common and knots are sometimes easily dislodged while you work. This is a better grade than #4 or #5, but is still prone to check.

#2 common – This grade should be free of knotholes, but still has its share of knots.

#1 common – This is the top quality of the regular board grades. It may have small knots and other insignificant imperfections, but should have no knotholes, and is a good choice for projects in which small defects are not important.

D select – This is the lowest quality of the better-grade boards.

C select – This grade may have a few small blemishes on one side, but should be almost perfect on the other. It is usually used for indoor work only.

#1 and #2 clear – These are the best and most expensive grades. Spend the money if you wish to, but don't waste it! Use these grades only for the finest indoor and outdoor projects.

In addition to being graded by quality, wood stock will be more or less "wet." Wetness refers to the amount of sap still left in the wood when you buy it. Newly cut lumber is quite wet and must be air or kiln dried (seasoned) before it can be used. There is always some sap left, but it should be a very small amount. Wood that is not sufficiently dry will warp, crack, and shrink much more than dried wood. Unfortunately, there is no sure way to assess the amount of sap still left in the wood, even though the dealer may assure you it has been kiln-dried. About the only hint we can give is to look at the end grain of each board (see **Figure A** again). Heartwood that is not sufficiently dry will become thinner as it loses moisture but is less likely to warp than sapwood.

When using lower grades of lumber, and consequently saving your bankroll, use your head as well. Buy a little extra so that you can eliminate the worst knots and cracks. You can repair the lumber by filling small cracks and gouges using wood putty or a mixture of glue and sawdust. Warped boards sometimes can be weighted and straightened, but be aware that this takes time. Tap all knots to see which ones will fall out, and then glue them back in place. If a board is badly checked at the ends it's best to cut off the cracked portion, because the cracks will eventually worsen, and

THE GREAT MECHANICAL WOODEN TOY BOOK

perhaps even split the entire board. Minor checking should be filled with wood putty in the same manner as cracks and gouges.

Finishes

PLEASE NOTE that no wooden toy should be left outdoors or otherwise exposed to the elements for any length of time no matter how it is finished. Most of the projects presented in this book are best suited to an indoor environment, and will last for generations with a minimum of care.

You may wish to paint some of the projects you make, but if you use any of the more attractive woods it seems a shame to cover the natural grain and color. In this case, you can obtain a good non-toxic finish by rubbing ordinary vegetable oil or olive oil into the wood. If you do paint, be certain to select a non-toxic paint. Small children will chew on anything and, believe it or not, wood doesn't taste half-bad.

Adhesive

We recommend both glue and fasteners (either nails, brads, or screws) for all joints, except those that must be free to rotate or pivot. For most projects in this book, we used aliphatic resin, commonly sold as carpenter's wood glue. For outdoor projects (such as the eagle whirligig), you'll need a waterproof glue. Be forewarned that the term is sometimes used loosely on product labels. We suggest that you use a marine glue or a two-part epoxy that must be mixed and used immediately. Waterproof glue also may be brushed on like paint to seal the end grain and prohibit water absorption. As a general rule, all glue assemblies should be clamped, but not so tightly as to force out most of the glue. Thirty minutes is sufficient clamping time for most joints. Those that will be under a great deal of stress should be clamped overnight. Joints secured with power-driven screws need not be clamped at all.

Fasteners and Other Hardware

Under normal conditions, ordinary hardware will suffice. However, if the toy will be exposed to the elements, you may wish to use hardware that is not subject to rust. Galvanized hardware is more rustproof, but better yet are fasteners made of brass, bronze, and alloyed stainless steel. If you can't find galvanized hardware, or don't wish to pay more for brass, bronze, or stainless, look for a rust-inhibiting product with which to coat steel hardware.

Screws should always be countersunk. This will prevent the possibility of little ones sustaining scratches caused by slightly protruding screw heads. In the same vein, finishing nails may be recessed but common nails usually are not. If you countersink the screws, the recesses may be filled with wooden plugs or wood filler. Wooden plugs will be almost invisible if you cut them from stock that matches the grain of the surrounding wood. This is easy to do, using a plug cutter (**Figure B**). Plugs can also be made by cutting slices from dowel rod, but they present end grain and will be much more apparent, particularly if the wood is stained.

Cutting and Joining

Butt Joints: A butt joint normally connects the end of one piece to the surface or edge of another (**Figure C**). The end grain of one piece will always show. Because there are no cuts made to form interlocking portions, this is an extemely weak joint. A butt joint can be

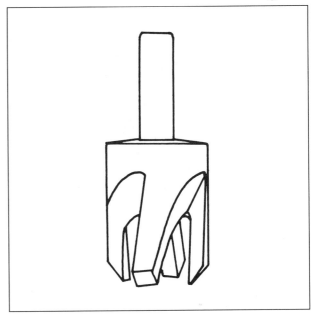

Figure C

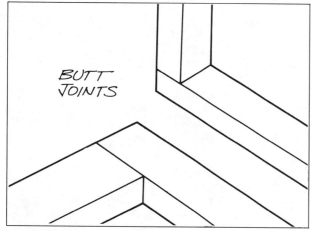

BUTT JOINTS

Figure D

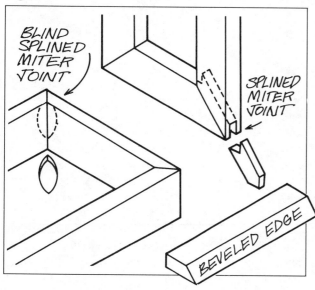

BLIND SPLINED MITER JOINT

SPLINED MITER JOINT

BEVELED EDGE

Figure E

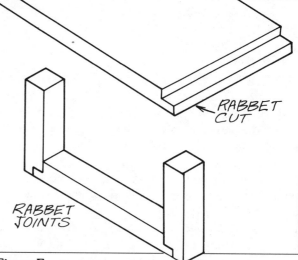

RABBET CUT

RABBET JOINTS

Figure F

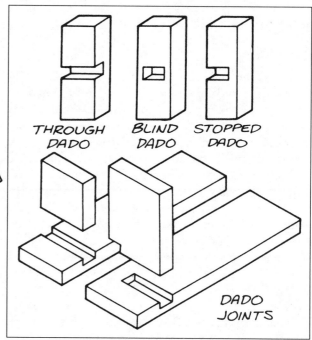

THROUGH DADO

BLIND DADO

STOPPED DADO

DADO JOINTS

strengthened using glue blocks, nails, screws, dowels, or other reinforcement.

Miters and Bevels: A miter joint connects two angle-cut ends (**Figure D**). It conceals the end grain of both pieces and can be reinforced using splines, dowels, or fasteners. The most common miter is a 45-degree, which is used to construct right-angle assemblies. A bevel is an angle cut made along an edge or surface.

Rabbets: A rabbet is an L-shaped groove and has many applications. A rabbet cut into one or both pieces to be joined conceals the end grain of one piece and

allows for a greater surface area to be glued, thus creating a stronger joint (**Figure E**). Normally it is reinforced using screws or nails.

Dado: Basically, a dado is a groove. Several types of dadoes and dado joints are illustrated in **Figure F**. A

THE GREAT MECHANICAL WOODEN TOY BOOK

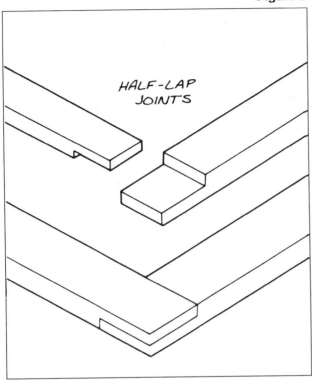

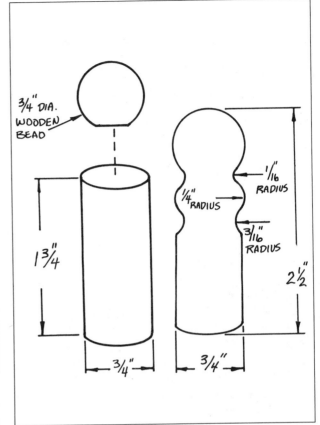

through dado extends all the way from edge to edge (or end to end). A stopped dado extends from one edge to a point short of the opposite edge. A blind dado is stopped short of both edges.

Lap Joints: A lap joint normally is used to connect two members at right angles. In the most common lap joint, the two joined surfaces are flush (**Figure G**). This joint provides a large area to be glued.

Toymaker's Secrets

Little Dowel People: Several of the projects in this book are designed to carry little play people, affectionately known as little dowel people. You can buy these little people in most hobby and craft shops, but here are a couple of ways to make them. If you feel like tinkering at your lathe, the dimensions of our little dowel person are provided in **Figure H**. You can also approximate the contours by mounting a length of ¾-inch-diameter dowel rod in a drill press and shaping it with sandpaper or a file. An even simpler method is to install a small

Figure I

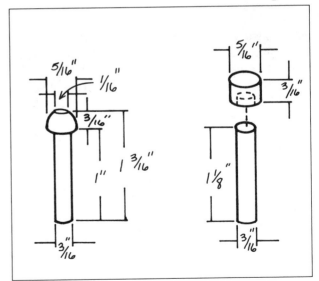

Figure J

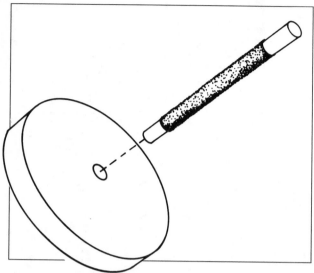

Figure K

wooden bead or drawer pull on one end of a length of dowel rod, as shown in **Figure H**.

Wooden Pegs: Craft shops carry a wide variety of small wooden pegs with caps that are almost indispensable to toymakers. In our projects they serve as everything from axle pegs to crank shafts; from connecting pins to train whistles. You can turn pegs yourself (if you've a mind to), or construct them from short lengths of dowel rod, as shown in **Figure I**. (And don't say we didn't warn you when you read the materials list for the freight train.)

Dealing with Dowel: For dowel rod crank and gear axles that are mounted in a larger support piece, you'll be assured of smoother operation by drilling a hole the same diameter as the dowel rod, and enlarging it slightly. One method is to sand a spare length of dowel, wrap it with sandpaper, and twist it around the sides of the hole a few times, as shown in **Figure J**.

Waste Allowance

We have specified the materials required to build each project in this book. Because you cannot use every single inch of stock, especially if you purchase a lower grade of wood, we have added a waste allowance of approximately ten percent to each material called for. Special instances in which a waste allowance is not included are noted. Although it may sound like

a fairly large amount, ten percent is not really a lot to allow for waste. Keep this in mind when you are at the lumberyard. We suggest that you initially purchase only enough stock to make one project, and note how much extra you have after all the parts are cut. This will give you a better basis on which to judge your purchases for subsequent projects.

Enlarging Scale Drawings

For unusually shaped or contoured parts, whenever possible we have provided full-size patterns or cutting diagrams that can be plotted directly on the wood using basic tools such as a square and angle measure. In some instances, however, we had to provide scale drawings, which are shown on a background grid of squares. Each small square on the grid is equal to a 1-inch square on the full-size part, and the drawing must be enlarged to make a full-size pattern. To enlarge a scale drawing you'll need a large piece of paper containing a grid of 1-inch squares. You can make your own pattern paper by drawing the 1-inch grid on brown wrapping paper, shelf paper, or flattened grocery bags, or you can purchase pattern paper that already contains the grid. It is available in at least two forms: as draft paper (check an art supply store) and as dressmaker's pattern paper. To enlarge the scale drawing simply reproduce the lines onto the paper containing the larger grid, working one square at a time (**Figure K**).

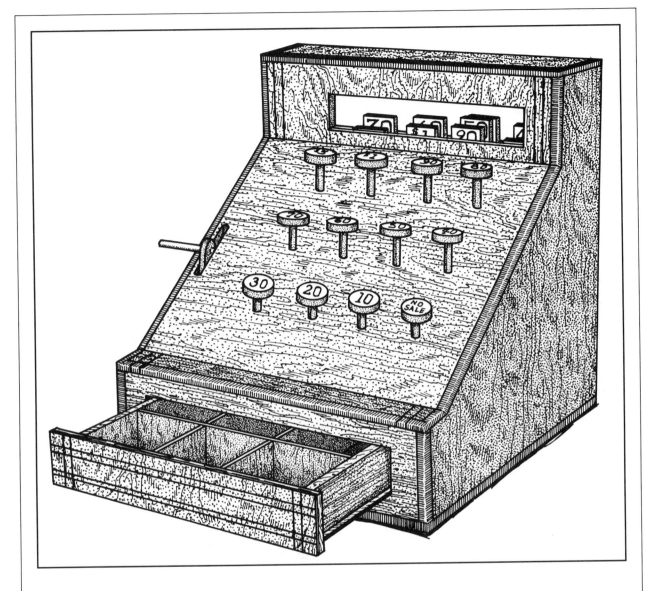

Cash Register

CLINK! DING! Ah, the sound of that cold, hard, cash! This 12 x 12 x 12-inch working model will bring out the entrepenurial spirit and help a budding tycoon learn to count the change. Perfect for playing store or for the ever-popular lemonaide stand—the keys and cash drawer really work!

Figure A

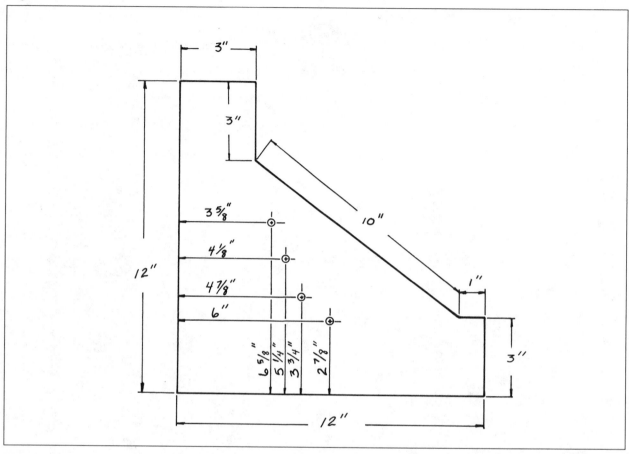

Materials

10 x 20-inch piece of ⅛-inch-thick interior plywood
3 x 3-foot piece of ¼-inch-thick interior plywood
3 linear feet of ⅛-inch-diameter wooden dowel rod
13 linear feet of ¼-inch-diameter wooden dowel rod
20 linear inches of ½-inch-diameter wooden dowel rod
3 linear feet of ¾-inch-diameter wooden dowel rod
5 linear inches of 1-inch-diameter wooden dowel rod
5 linear feet of pine 1 x 2
3 linear feet of 2 x 4
Scrap piece of 2 x 4, approximately 6 inches long
No. 18 wire brads, each ¾ inch long
Seven No. 4 gauge oval-head screws, each ½ inch long
One No. 6 gauge flathead screw, 1 inch long
Seven heavy-duty rubber bands

Cutting the Shell Pieces

1. For the shell of the cash register, cut the pieces listed here from ¼-inch plywood. Label each piece as it's cut to avoid confusion later.

Code	Quantity	Dimensions
A	3	3 x 12 inches
B	1	10 x 12 inches
C	1	1½ x 12 inches
D	1	12 x 12¼ inches
E	1	12 x 12½ inches
F	2	12 x 12 inches
G	1	2¾ x 11½ inches

Figure B

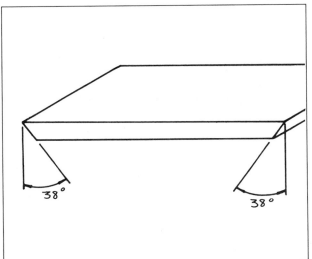

Figure C

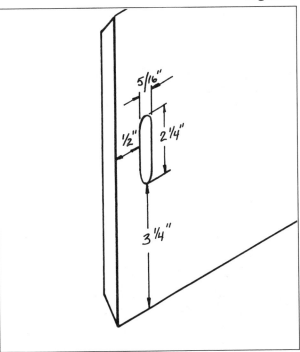

2. A cutting diagram for the F Side pieces is provided in **Figure A**. Cut two Sides from the rectangular pieces you cut in step 1. The Sides must be drilled to accommodate support rods for the key mechanism. To insure that the holes will line up exactly, place the two Side pieces on top of each other to drill the holes. Where indicated in **Figure A**, drill a ⁵⁄₁₆-inch-diameter hole through one Side, and continue drilling to make a socket ³⁄₁₆-inch deep at the corresponding point in the remaining Side.

3. Bevel both long edges of the B Keyboard at a 38-degree angle, as shown in **Figure B**. Cut a ⁵⁄₁₆ x 2¼-inch slot in the Keyboard, 3¼ inches from one beveled edge and ½ inch from one short edge, as shown in **Figure C**. Round off the ends of the slot.

4. One A piece will serve as the "window" of the cash register. Bevel one long edge of the A piece at a 38-degree angle, as shown in **Figure D**. In addition, cut a 1¼ x 7¾-inch slot, 1¼ inches from the unbeveled edge and 3 inches from one short edge (**Figure E**).

5. Bevel one long edge of the C piece at a 38-degree angle, as shown in **Figure D**.

6. One A piece will serve as the front of the cash register, so it must have an opening for the cash drawer. In the center of the A piece, cut a 1½ x 9½-inch slot, as shown in **Figure F**.

Figure D

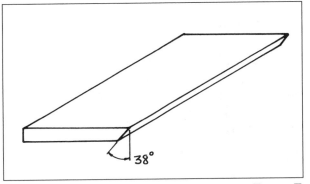

Figure E

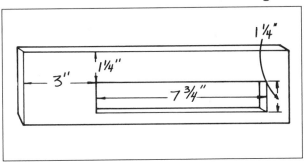

Figure F

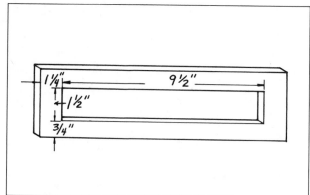

Figure G

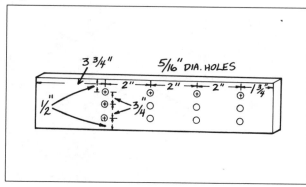

Figure H

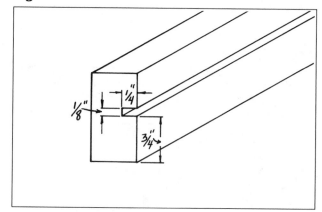

2. Cut a ⅛ x ¼-inch groove along one long edge of each H Drawer Slide, ¾ inch from the lower edge, as shown in **Figure H**.

3. The M and N Drawer Dividers are slotted to fit together. Cut a ⅛ x ¾-inch groove in each M Divider, 2¾ inches from one end, as shown in **Figure I**. In addition, cut two of the same size slot in the N Divider, spacing them 2⅝ inches from each end.

4. We beveled the K Drawer Facer at a slight angle toward all four edges, as shown in **Figure J**. Avoid beveling the entire thickness of the board.

Cutting the Key Mechanism Pieces

1. For the key mechanism, cut the lengths of dowel rod listed here from the dowel diameter indicated.

Code	Quantity	Length	Dowel
O	4	2 inches	¼-inch
P	4	3½ inches	¼-inch
Q	4	5 inches	¼-inch
R	4	3¼ inches	½-inch
S	4	6 inches	½-inch
T	4	8⅞ inches	½-inch
U	12	2⅜ inches	¼-inch
V	12	¼ inch	1-inch
W	3	13 inches	¼-inch
X	3	3½ inches	¾-inch
Y	12	1½ inches	¾-inch
Z	3	8 inches	¼-inch

7. The G piece must be drilled to accommodate the shafts that connect the price tabs to the inner mechanism. Drill twelve ⁵⁄₁₆-inch-diameter holes, spacing them ¾ inch apart in rows, with 2 inches between rows, as shown in **Figure G**.

Cutting the Drawer Pieces

1. For the drawer, cut the pieces listed here from the materials indicated, and label each piece.

Code	Quantity	Dimensions	Material
H	2	1½ x 9¼ inches	1 x 2
I	1	1¼ x 9½ inches	¼-inch plywood
J	3	1¼ x 9 inches	¼-inch plywood
K	1	2 x 10 inches	¼-inch plywood
L	1	9½ x 9½ inches	⅛-inch plywood
M	2	1⅜ x 9 inches	⅛-inch plywood
N	1	1⅜ x 8⅜ inches	⅛-inch plywood

Figure I

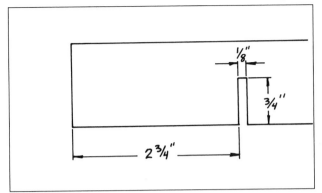

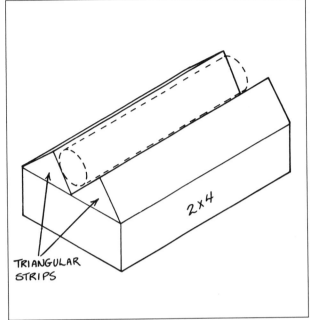

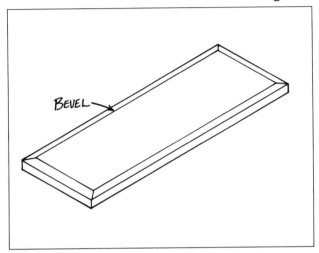

BEVEL

TRIANGULAR STRIPS

2 x 4

Figure L

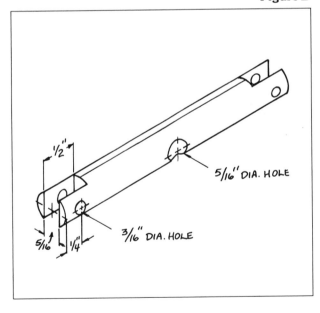

5/16" DIA. HOLE

3/16" DIA. HOLE

2. Each of the Pivot shafts (R, S, and T pieces) must be slotted and drilled on both ends to accommodate the Tab shafts (O, P, and Q pieces) and Key shafts (U pieces), as shown in **Figure L**. To make the monumental task of cutting the uniform slots a (s)lot easier, we built a dowel jig (**Figure K**). To build the jig, cut a 6-inch length of 1 x 2 in half along the diagonal. Mount the two triangular pieces on a scrap piece of 2 x 4, butting the edges as shown in **Figure K**. To cut slots in one Pivot shaft, place it in the jig, and draw a line along one side of the dowel with a pencil. In one end, cut a slot 5/16 inch wide and 1/2 inch deep, centered on the line, as shown in **Figure L**. Cut an identical slot in the opposite end, also centered on the line. Cut identical slots in both ends of each Pivot shaft.

3. Drill a 3/16-inch-diameter hole through each Pivot shaft, 1/4 inch from each end, as shown in **Figure L**. In addition, drill a 5/16-inch-diameter hole through the mid-point of each Pivot shaft, as shown.

Figure M

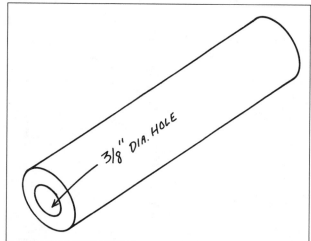

Figure N

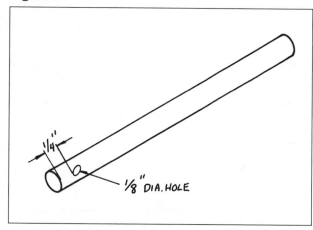

Figure O

Cutting the Drawer Mechanism Pieces

1. The drawer mechanism consists of two Handle pieces, a drawer Catch, and a Pivot Block. All of these pieces are cut from 1 x 2. To cut the Handle and Catch pieces, rip a ⅜-inch-wide strip, approximately 20 inches long, from the wider board. From the strip, cut two Handle pieces, one 5⅝ inches, and one 6⅜ inches long (save the remainder of the strip). The two pieces will be attached at a right angle, using a lap joint. Cut a ³⁄₁₆ x ¾-inch lap in one end of each Handle piece, as shown in **Figure P**. Drill a ¼-inch-diameter hole through the shorter Handle piece, ⅜ inch from the end opposite the lap cut, to accommodate the handle grip (**Figure P**). In addition, round off the handle grip end of the shorter Handle piece, as shown. Drill a ¼-inch-diameter hole through the longer Handle piece, ¼ inch from the end opposite the lap cut (**Figure P**). In addition, drill a ⁵⁄₁₆-inch-diameter hole through the longer piece, 4 inches from the same (drilled) end (**Figure P**).

4. Drill a ⅜-inch-diameter hole through the length of each X and Y piece, as shown in **Figure M**.

5. Drill a ⅛-inch-diameter hole through each O, P, Q and U piece, ¼ inch from one end, to accommodate a wooden pin (**Figure N**).

6. For the price tabs, rip a ⅜-inch-wide strip from the 2 x 4, approximately 35 inches long. Cut the strip down to 1¼ inches wide. Cut eight tabs, each 1¾ inches long, and four tabs, each 2 inches long. Drill a ¼-inch-diameter socket, ¼ inch deep, centered in the bottom edge of each tab, as shown in **Figure O**.

7. Drill a shallow ¼-inch-diameter socket in the center of each V Key to accommodate the key shaft.

2. A full-size pattern for the Catch is provided in **Figure Q**. Cut the Catch from the remaining length of the strip you cut in step 1, and drill a ³⁄₁₆-inch-diameter hole through it, as shown.

3. A full-size pattern for the Pivot Block is provided in **Figure Q**. Cut the Block from 1 x 2. Cut the slot in the Block, as shown, and drill a ⅛-inch-diameter hole through the Block, 1¾ inches from the upper end.

4. Cut two lengths of ¼-inch-diameter dowel rod to serve as the handle Grip and Catch Release. The Grip is 2⅛ inches long; the Release, 3 inches long. Cut a 1-inch length of ¼-inch-diameter dowel rod to serve as the Handle Pivot. Drill a ⅛-inch-diameter hole through the Pivot, ¼ inch from one end. In addition, cut a 1-inch square of ¼-inch plywood to use as a Spacer in the drawer release mechanism.

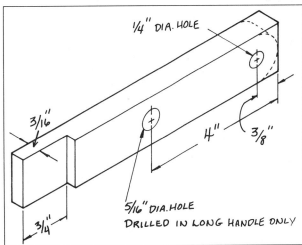

Figure P

Figure Q

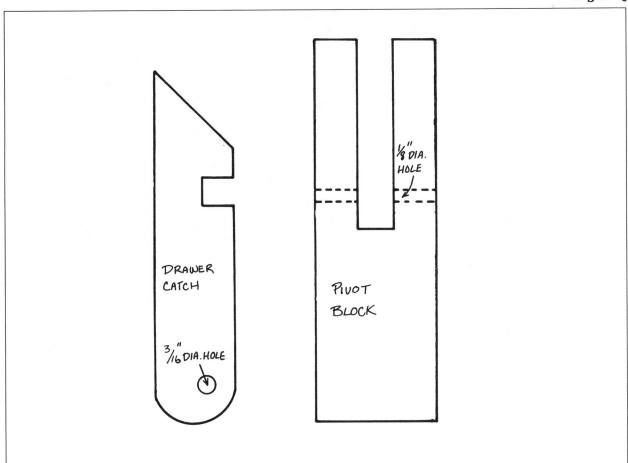

Figure R

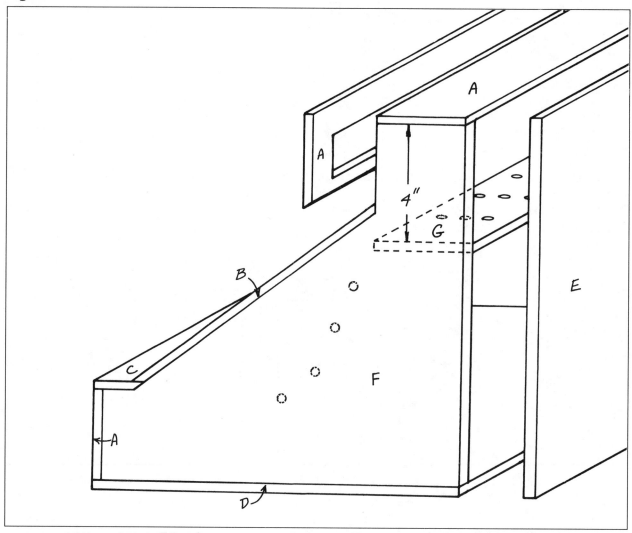

Assembling the Shell

1. The assembled shell is shown in **Figure R**. To begin, attach the drilled F piece to the left-hand side of the D piece, with the rear edges flush, as shown. Attach the remaining F piece to the opposite side of the D piece in the same manner, with the sockets facing toward the other F piece. Attach the unslotted A piece so that it covers the upper edges of the F pieces, as shown. Attach the drawer-slotted A piece along the front edge of the D piece, and attach the C piece so that it covers the upper edge of the A piece, as shown. Attach the B piece, butting the lower edge against the C piece as shown. The ends of the A, B, and C pieces should be even with the F pieces. Wait to attach the window-slotted A piece until you've installed the key mechanism.

2. Attach the G piece between the F Sides, with the holes on the left-hand end, as shown in **Figure R**. The G piece should be placed 4 inches below the underside of the top A piece, and flush with the back edges of the Sides, as shown.

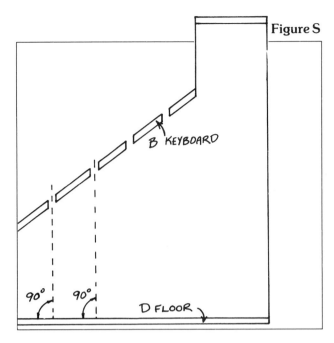

Figure S

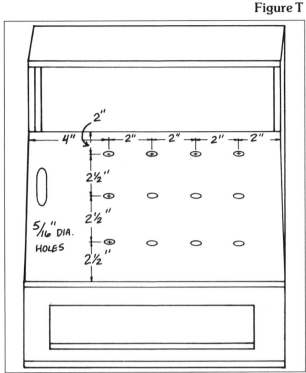

Figure T

3. The holes for the shafts that connect the keys to the mechanism inside must be drilled through the keyboard (B piece) at a 90-degree angle to the floor of the cash register, as shown in **Figure S**. Use a drill press, or hold your drill as straight as possible, and drill twelve 5/16-inch-diameter holes, spacing them 2 inches apart in rows, with 2½ inches between rows, as shown in **Figure T**.

4. Install the H Drawer Slides so that the groove is located in the lower corner of the drawer opening in the A piece, as shown in **Figure U**.

Assembling the Drawer

1. The drawer joints are secured using glue and brads. The assembled drawer is shown in **Figure V**. To begin, assemble the Sides, Front, and Back (I and J pieces), as shown. Center the assembled drawer box over the L Floor, so that ¼ inch of the Floor extends beyond each Side. Attach the K Facer so that it extends ¼ inch beyond all four edges of the Front, as shown.

2. Install the M and N Dividers as shown in **Figure V**. The M Dividers run from front to back; the N Divider runs across the drawer.

3. Install a cup hook in the middle of the drawer Back, as shown.

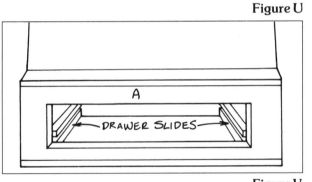

Figure U

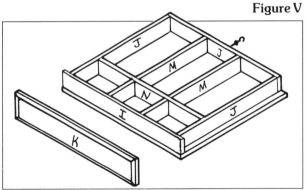

Figure V

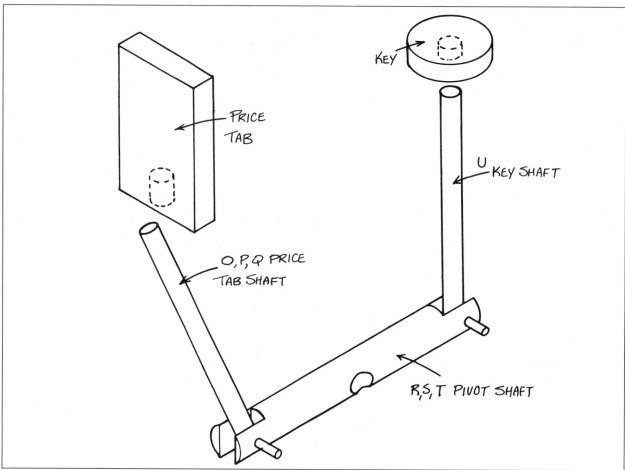

PRICE TAB

KEY

U KEY SHAFT

O, P, Q PRICE TAB SHAFT

R, S, T PIVOT SHAFT

Assembling the Key Mechanism

1. Each key on the cash register is connected by three shafts to a price tab, as shown in **Figure W**. To build one key assembly, install one **U** Key Shaft on one end of an **R**, **S**, or **T** Pivot Shaft, using a 1-inch length of ⅛-inch-diameter dowel rod as a pin (**Figure W**). On the opposite end of the Pivot Shaft, install a Price Tab Shaft in the same manner, as shown. The key and price tab shafts should hang loosely on the pivot shafts, so the assembly will operate smoothly.

2. Build eleven additional key assemblies in the same manner. You should end up with three different lengths of key assemblies, and four assemblies of each length.

3. Each key assembly pivots on a Support Rod that runs between the sides of the cash register, as shown in **Figure X**. Begin with the top row, using the four shortest key assemblies. Slide one **W** Support Rod through the top hole in the side of the cash register. Working from inside the shell, slide one **X** Long Spacer on the support shaft as shown. Slip the Pivot Shaft of one key assembly on the Support Rod, then add a **Y** Short Spacer, as shown. Slip three remaining key assemblies of the same length on the support shaft, placing short spacers between them, as shown. Slip one additional Short Spacer on the end of the Support Rod. Insert the end of the Support Rod into the top socket on the opposite side of the cash register. Turn the key

Figure X

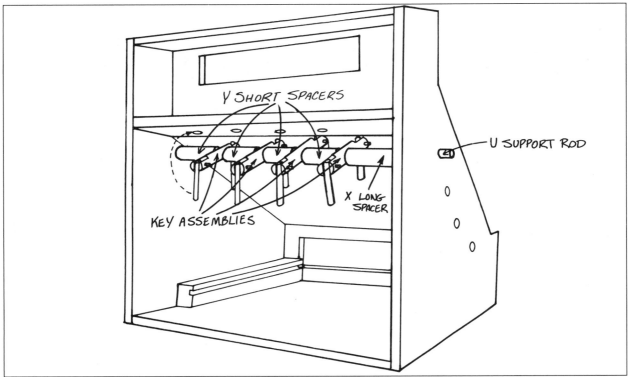

and price tab shafts upwards so that the ends engage in the holes in the keyboard and **G** piece, as shown.

4. Install the two remaining Support Rods and key assemblies in the same manner. Insert a screw through the socket side of the cash register into the end of each Support Rod to hold it securely in place.

5. The action of the key mechanism is provided by rubber bands connected between the floor of the cash register and a length of dowel (**Z** piece) that rests on top of the pivot shafts, as shown in **Figure Y**. Install the upper dowel first, placing the rubber bands between the key assemblies as shown. We didn't find it essential, but you can cut a small groove to hold the rubber bands in place on the dowel rod. Install the rubber bands and dowel rods on the middle and lower rows, then insert two cup hooks in the floor of the cash register. Hook the rubber bands over the cup hooks as shown.

6. After you've installed the key mechanism, install the window-slotted **A** piece, butting the edges as shown in **Figure R**.

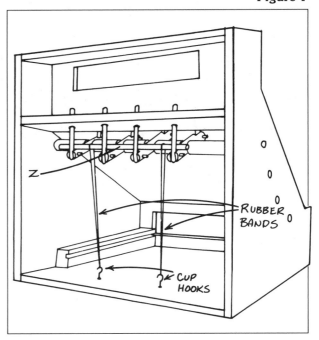

Figure Z

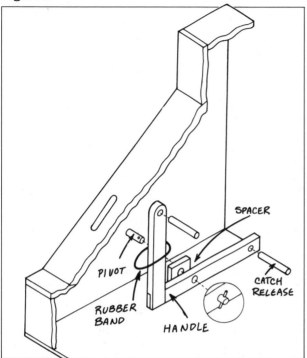

Figure BB

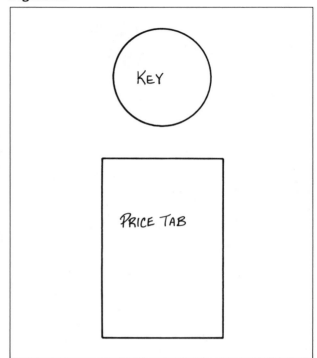

Figure AA

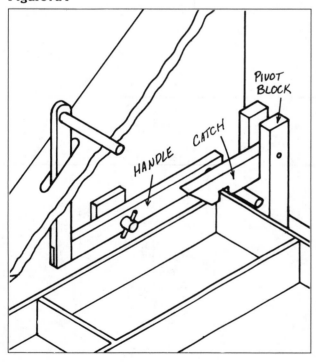

Assembling the Drawer Mechanism

1. Assemble the drawer mechanism Handle using the laps you cut in the pieces earlier. Slip a rubber band around the Handle (it won't be as easy to add once the Handle is installed). To install the Handle, insert the Pivot into the lowest hole in the cash register side, as shown in **Figure Z**, and glue it in place. Working from inside the shell, slip the Spacer over the Pivot, as shown. Slip the Handle over the Pivot, inserting the upper end into the slot in the keyboard of the cash register, as shown. Insert a 1-inch length of ⅛-inch-diameter dowel in the hole in the Pivot, as shown.

2. Attach the Drawer Catch to the Pivot Block, using a 1-inch length of ⅛-inch-diameter dowel rod as a pin, as shown in **Figure AA**.

3. Glue the Catch Release in the lower Handle hole, as shown in **Figure AA**. Insert the drawer, and slide it closed. Position the drawer catch assembly so that the slot in the Catch engages over the back of the drawer, as shown in **Figure AA**. Secure the Pivot Block with a screw inserted up through the floor of the cash register.

Figure CC

No Sale	$5	$1
90¢	80¢	70¢
60¢	50¢	40¢
30¢	20¢	10¢

4. Glue the Grip in the upper Handle hole. Hold the rubber band with your finger inside the shell, and adjust the tension so that the handle is held in the "up" position. Install a cup hook on the side, and hook the rubber band to it.

Finishing Touches

1. Full-size patterns for the keys are provided in **Figure BB**. Corresponding patterns for the price tabs are provided in **Figure CC**. Paint or draw the numbers on the keys and tabs using non-toxic paints or markers. Install the tabs and keys – be sure to glue them on securely so they won't find their way into a child's mouth.

2. Cut four glue blocks from ¼-inch plywood and attach them flush with the edges of the back of the cash register in each corner. Attach the E Back so that it covers all of the rear edges, and secure it with screws inserted through the glue blocks.

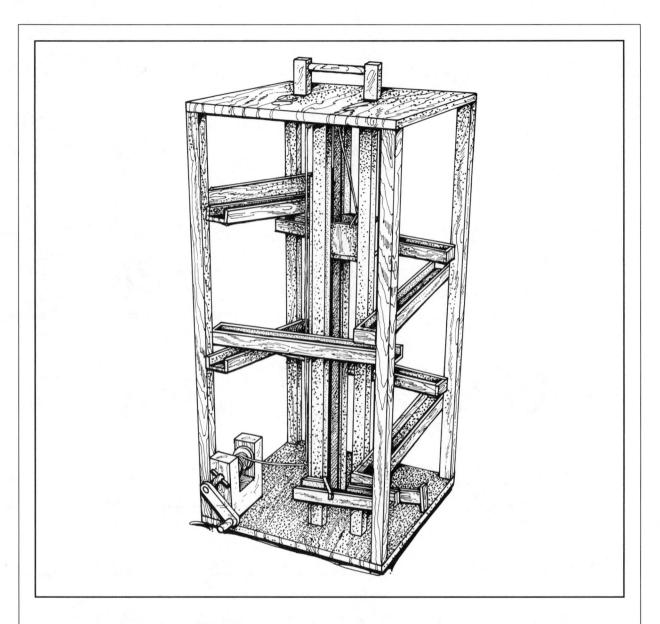

Magical Motion Machine

As addictive as a video game! This little wonder keeps children of all ages mesmerized as they crank the lift to the top, then watch the silver balls race down the chutes. Overall dimensions: 12 x 12 x 24 inches.

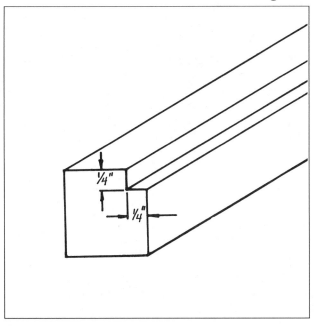

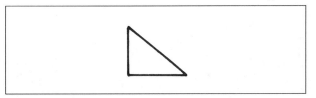

Materials

12 x 24-inch piece of ½-inch-thick interior grade plywood

10 x 24-inch piece of ¼-inch-thick interior grade plywood

5-foot length of pine 1 x 10. Part of this wood will be ripped into ¼-inch-wide strips to build the chutes. If you prefer, you can cut the strips from 1½ x ¼-inch lattice. In that case, you'll need approximately 12 linear feet of lattice, and a 3-foot length of 1 x 10.

4-inch length of pine 2 x 6

2-inch length of ⅛-inch-diameter wooden dowel rod

14-inch length of ⅜-inch-diameter wooden dowel rod

1⅞-inch length of ¾-inch-diameter wooden dowel rod

1-inch length of 1½-inch-diameter wooden closet rod

50-inch length of string

Five or more steel balls or marbles, each ⅝ inch in diameter

No. 18 wire brads, each ¾ inch long

No. 6 gauge flathead wood screws, each 1 inch long

Four eye screws, each ¾ inch long

Carpenter's wood glue, stain or paint, and beeswax (We used red, yellow, and blue paints.)

Cutting the Pieces

1. The frame consists of Top and Bottom plywood pieces and Supports ripped from 1 x 10. For the Top and Bottom, cut the piece of ½-inch plywood in half so you have two 12-inch squares. To make the Supports, cut a 24-inch length of 1 x 10 and rip it into eight ¾-inch-wide strips, each 24 inches long. Four Supports will serve as the elevator shaft. Cut a ¼ x ¼-inch rabbet along one long edge of these four Supports, as shown in **Figure A**. For the carrying handle, cut two ¾ x ¾ x 2-inch Handle pieces from 1 x 10, and a 4-inch length of ⅜-inch-diameter wooden dowel. Drill a ⅜-inch-diameter socket in each 2-inch Handle piece, ½ inch from one end.

2. For the lift box, cut the pieces listed here from ¼-inch plywood. A full-size pattern for the Corner Spacer is provided in **Figure B**.

Description	Quantity	Dimensions
Side	2	2 x 2¼ inches
Back	1	1¾ x 2 inches
Floor	1	1¾ x 2⅞ inches
Bottom	1	2¼ x 2¼ inches
Floor Support	1	1 x 1¾ inches
Corner Spacer	1	(see Figure B)

3. There are seven long chutes and two short ones. Cut the Floors from ¼-inch plywood. You can cut the remaining pieces from ¼-inch lattice or from ¼-inch strips ripped from 1 x 10. For the long chutes, cut the pieces listed here.

Description	Quantity	Dimensions
Floor	7	¼ x 1 x 12 inches
Side	14	¼ x ¾ x 12 inches
End	7	¾ x ¼ x 1½ inches
Spacer	7	½ x ½ x 1 inches

Figure C

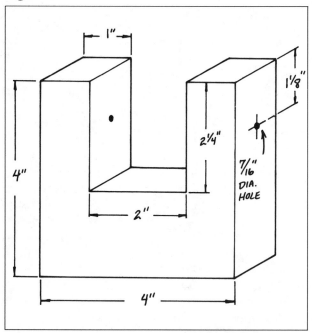

For the short chutes, cut the pieces listed here.

Description	Quantity	Dimensions
Floor	2	$\frac{1}{4}$ x 1 x $6\frac{1}{2}$ inches
Side	4	$\frac{1}{4}$ x $\frac{3}{4}$ x $6\frac{1}{2}$ inches
End	1	$\frac{1}{4}$ x $\frac{3}{4}$ x $1\frac{1}{2}$ inches
End Spacer	1	$\frac{1}{2}$ x $\frac{1}{2}$ x 1 inches
Guide Block	1	$\frac{1}{4}$ x $\frac{1}{2}$ x 2 inches
Side Spacer	1	$\frac{1}{4}$ x $\frac{1}{2}$ x 3 inches
Ramp	1	$\frac{1}{4}$ x $\frac{3}{4}$ x $1\frac{3}{4}$ inches

4. The crank assembly consists of a Support Block and Shaft with Handle and Spool. To begin, rip the length of 2 x 6 down to a 4-inch width. A cutting diagram for the notch in the Support Block is provided in **Figure C**. Cut the notch and drill a $\frac{7}{16}$-inch-diameter hole through each extension of the Support, centered $1\frac{1}{8}$ inches from the upper end. For the crank Handle, cut a $\frac{3}{8}$ x $\frac{3}{4}$ x 3-inch piece from 1 x 10. Round off the ends of the Handle, and drill a $\frac{3}{8}$-inch-diameter hole centered $\frac{3}{8}$ inch from each end. The additional crank pieces are cut from $\frac{3}{8}$, $\frac{3}{4}$, and $1\frac{1}{2}$-inch-diameter dowel. Cut the pieces listed here.

Figure D

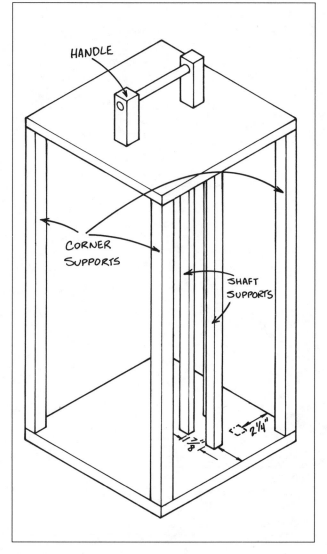

Description	Quantity	Length	Dowel
Shaft	1	6 inches	$\frac{3}{8}$-inch
Grip	1	$1\frac{1}{2}$ inches	$\frac{3}{8}$-inch
Spool Hub	1	$1\frac{7}{8}$ inches	$\frac{3}{4}$-inch
Spool End	2	$\frac{1}{8}$ inch	$1\frac{1}{2}$-inch

Assembling the Frame

1. The assembled frame is shown in **Figure D**. All of the Supports are secured with screws inserted through

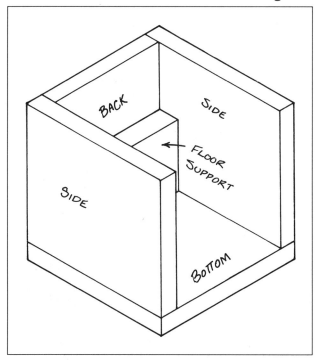

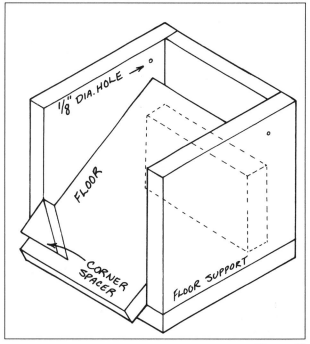

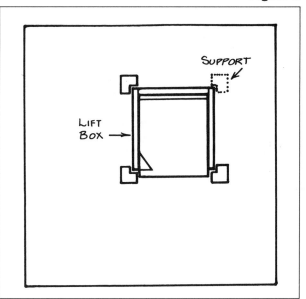

the Top and Bottom into the Support ends. To begin, install the four corner Supports as shown (**Figure D**). Install the carrying Handle on top of the frame, as shown. Install three of the elevator shaft Supports as shown, rotating each one so that the rabbet faces the inside of the shaft. Wait to install the fourth shaft until you've built and installed the lift box.

2. The assembled lift box is shown in **Figure E**. To begin, assemble the Sides, Back, and Bottom, butting the edges as shown. The Side and Bottom pieces should cover the edges of the Back. Attach the Support to the Back, inside the box, as shown. Attach the Floor so that one end butts against the Back and the remaining end overhangs the Bottom piece (**Figure F**). To insure that the balls will roll smoothly out of the lift into the first chute, attach the Corner Spacer to the lower front left-hand corner of the Floor, as shown in **Figure F**. Drill a ⅛-inch-diameter hole through each Side near the top, so you can attach a string to the box.

3. Position the assembled lift box at the bottom of the elevator shaft so that the corners engage in the rabbets

and the box floor fits between two Supports, as shown in **Figure G**. Install the remaining Support to complete the elevator shaft (**Figure G**).

Figure H

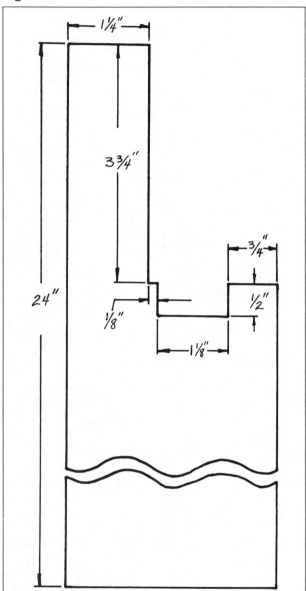

Figure I

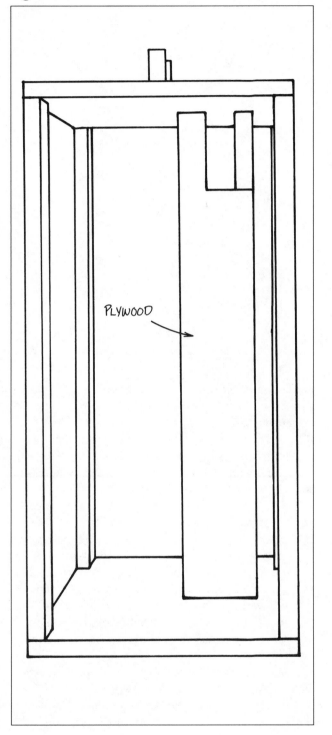

PLYWOOD

4. Cut a piece of ¼-inch plywood, 3¼ x 24 inches. This piece will fit over one side of the elevator shaft to keep the balls from rolling out of the lift box before it reaches the top. A cutting diagram for the notch at the upper end is provided in **Figure H**. Cut the notch and install the piece over one side of the elevator shaft, as shown in **Figure I**.

THE GREAT MECHANICAL WOODEN TOY BOOK

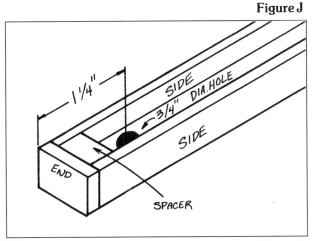

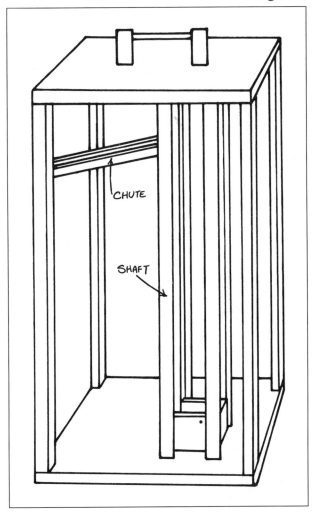

Figure K

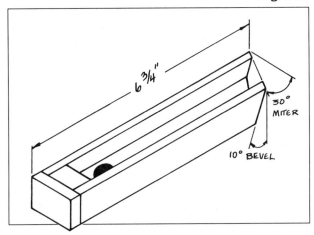

Assembling the Chutes

1. One assembled chute is shown in **Figure J**. Nail and glue the Sides to the Floor, butting the edges as shown. The edges of the Floor piece should be covered by the Sides. To avoid splitting the plywood, use only two brads in each Side. Attach the End and Spacer pieces to one end of the chute, butting the edges as shown. The ends of the Floor and Sides are covered by the End piece.

2. Drill a ¾-inch-diameter hole through the chute Floor, centered 1¼ inches from the end, as shown in **Figure J**.

3. Repeat the steps in this section to build eight additional chutes. Note: Two of the chutes are shorter than the others; these will be installed at the top and bottom of the structure. Do not drill one of the short chutes. (We dare you to repeat that tongue twister three times!)

Installing the Chutes

1. The first (short) chute at the top must be mitered and beveled as shown in **Figure K**. Miter the drilled short chute at a 30-degree angle, 6¾ inches from the drilled end (**Figure K**). Bevel the same end of the chute at a 10-degree angle, as shown. Install the chute, butting the mitered end against the elevator shaft, as shown in **Figure L**.

Figure M

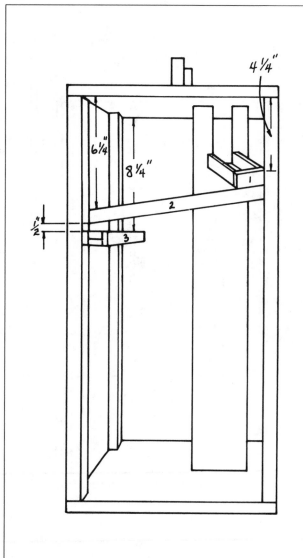

Figure N

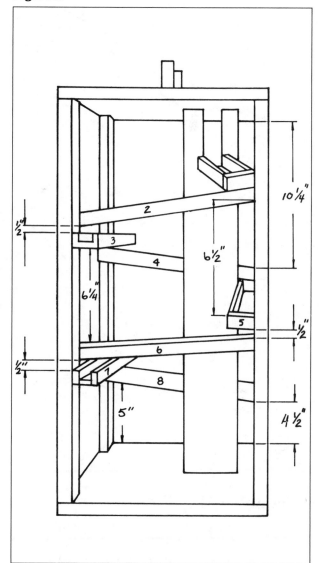

2. Install the second chute as shown in **Figure M**, butting the upper edges against the underside of the first chute. Position the lower end of the chute 6¼ inches below the frame top and nail it in place (**Figure M**). Place the entire structure on a flat surface and test the action of the chutes by rolling a ball down them a few times. Make adjustments to the spacers and chutes so that the ball rolls down the chutes without getting stuck or falling out.

3. Install the third chute below the second one, allowing ½ inch between them (**Figure M**). Position the chute with the lower end 8¼ inches below the top, and nail in place. Test the action.

4. Install the fourth, fifth, sixth, seventh, and eighth chutes as shown in **Figure N**. Allow ½ inch between chutes, as shown. Position the lower end of the fourth chute 10¼ inches below the top, as shown. Position the lower end of the fifth chute 6½ inches below the

THE GREAT MECHANICAL WOODEN TOY BOOK

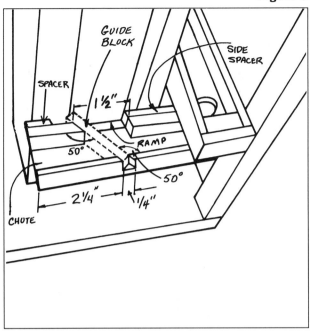

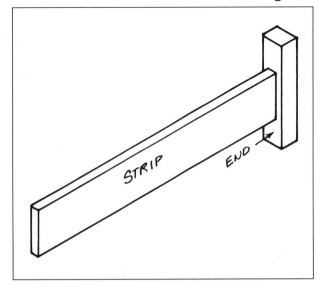

lower end of the second chute, as shown. Position the lower end of the sixth chute 6¼ inches below the upper end of the third chute, as shown. Install the eighth chute next, and position the upper end 5 inches above the frame bottom, and the lower end 4½ inches above the bottom. Install the seventh chute so that the upper end is ½ inch below the sixth chute and the lower end is ½ inch above the eighth chute, as shown.

5. The last (undrilled) chute will hold the balls in single file until you release them into the lowered lift box. Most of the modifications to the chute are done after it is installed on the structure, as shown in **Figure O**. To install the chute, cut a ⅛-inch-wide spacer from pine, and attach it to one support of the elevator shaft, 2⅞ inches from the bottom of the frame. Attach one end of the chute ½ inch below the eighth chute, and the lower end to the spacer on the elevator shaft, as shown. Using a hand saw, cut a ¼-inch slot through both sides of the chute at a 50-degree angle (**Figure O**). To make an opening for the balls to roll out of the chute, cut a 1½-inch notch in one side of the chute, as shown. Attach the Guide Block across the chute floor at the lower end of the side opening, as shown. Attach the

Side Spacer along one side of the chute. Attach the Ramp between two corners of the elevator shaft, just below the side opening in the chute, as shown.

6. To make the ball release handle (**Figure P**), rip a ¹⁄₁₆-inch-thick strip from 1 x 10, 4¾ inches long. Cut a ¼ x ⅜ x 1¾-inch end piece. Cut a ¹⁄₁₆-inch notch in the center of the end piece, insert the strip, and glue it in place, as shown (**Figure P**).

7. To build the two handle supports, rip approximately 4 inches of ¼-inch-thick pine from a wider board. Cut the strip down to ¼ inch wide. From this strip, cut two 1¼-inch lengths, and four ⅜-inch lengths. Use these lengths to construct the two supports, butting the ends as shown in **Figure Q**. Glue each assembled support to the inner side of the bottom chute, as shown.

The Crank Assembly

1. A view of the crank is shown in **Figure R**. To begin, insert the Grip in one of the Handle holes. Secure it by inserting a pin cut from ⅛-inch-diameter dowel through a small hole drilled through the side of the Handle into the Grip (**Figure R**). Insert the Shaft in the remaining Handle hole, so that it extends the opposite direction from the Grip, as shown. Secure it in the same manner.

Figure Q

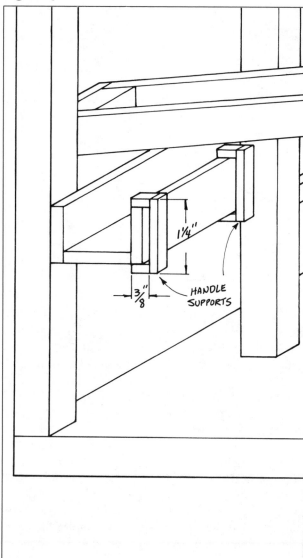

Figure R

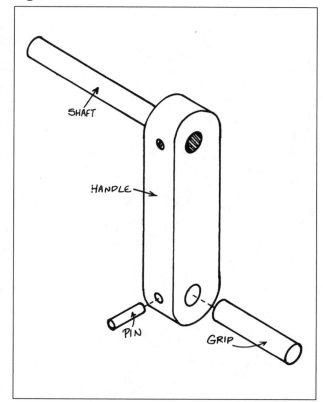

Figure S

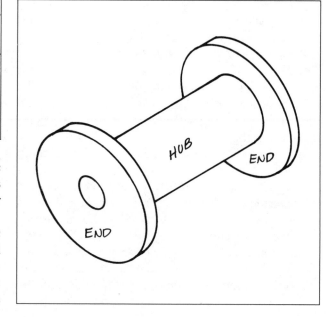

2. The spool is shown in **Figure S**. To begin, glue one Spool End to each end of the Spool Hub, as shown. Drill a ⅜-inch-diameter hole through the center of the assembled spool, as shown.

3. Insert the crank shaft through one prong of the support piece, as shown in **Figure T**. Slide the spool over the shaft, then slip the shaft into the opposite support piece prong, as shown. Adjust the spool on the shaft so that it turns easily without binding on the sides

THE GREAT MECHANICAL WOODEN TOY BOOK

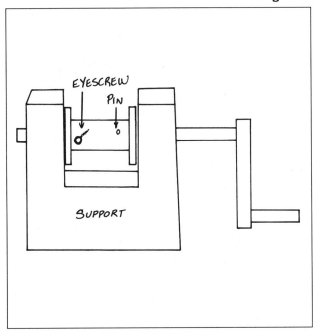

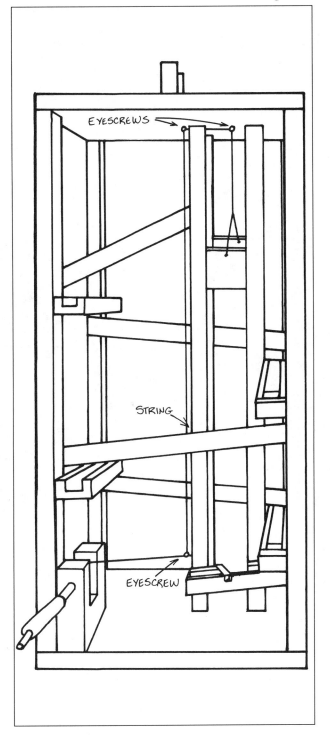

of the support piece prongs. Drill a ⅛-inch-diameter hole through the spool and shaft, and insert a pin cut from ⅛-inch-diameter dowel (**Figure T**). Install an eye screw approximately ½ inch from one end of the spool, as shown.

Final Assembly

1. Install the crank assembly by inserting screws up through the bottom of the frame, butting the edges as shown in **Figure U**.

2. Install the eyescrews on the underside of the top piece and on the lift shaft, as shown in **Figure U**. The eyescrew over the elevator shaft should be centered. Be sure to place the remaining eyescrews so that the string will not rub against any wooden parts.

3. Tie one end of the string to the lift box, using the holes in the sides, as shown in **Figure U**. Thread the free end of the string through the eyescrews, and tie it to the eyescrew on the crank.

4. Lubricate the inside edges of the elevator shaft with beeswax.

5. Load the balls into the lift box, crank away, and let the good times roll!

Chirpin' Chicks

These hilarious cluckers are off their axles! Youngsters from one to ninety-one will cackle with delight as Mother Hen and her fowlish family strut by, bobbing from side to side. The secret to creating this birdly behavior is drilling the wheel holes off-center.

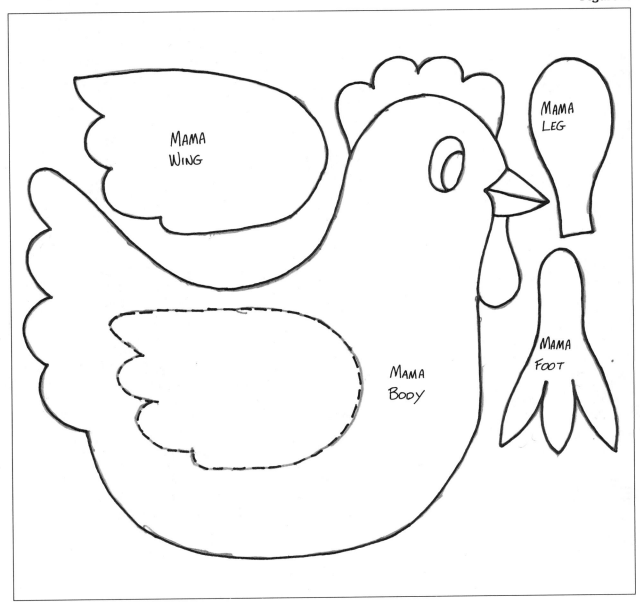

MAMA
WING

MAMA
LEG

MAMA
BODY

MAMA
FOOT

Materials

6-inch length of 2 x 8-inch clear pine lumber
16-inch length of 1 x 8-inch clear pine lumber
21-inch length of ¼ x 1¾-inch wooden lattice
40 square inches of ½-inch thick pine lumber, at least
   2 inches wide

3-foot length of ¼-inch diameter wooden dowel rod
6-foot length of cotton cord, ¼ inch or less in diameter
Finishing nails: two 1 inch long, two ¾ inch long, and
   fourteen ½ inch long
Carpenter's wood glue, wood filler, and paint in your
   choice of colors

Figure B

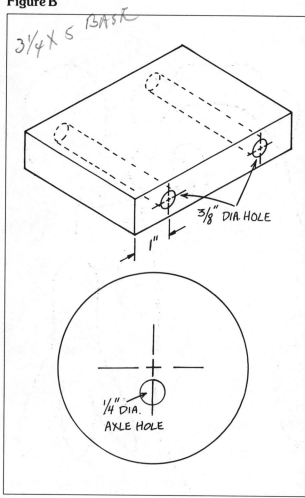

Figure C

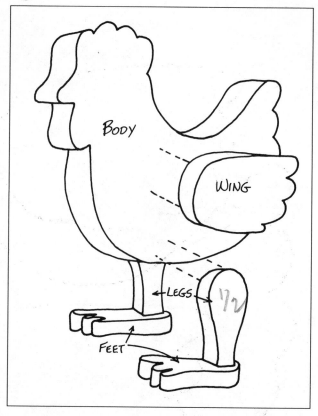

Tools

Saber saw (or coping saw), hammer, wood rasp, nailset, electric or hand drill, and drill bits of the following diameters: ¼-inch and ⅜-inch

A circle-cutting drill attachment will help you cut the wheels.

MAMA
Cutting the pieces

1. Full-size patterns for the pieces required to build Mama Chicken are given in **Figure A.** Make a kraft paper pattern for each piece.

2. Cut one Body from the pine 2 x 8, and two Feet from the lattice. Cut one Base, 3¼ x 5 inches, and two Wings from the pine 1 x 8. Cut four Wheels, each 2 inches in diameter, and two Legs from the ½-inch thick lumber. Sand each piece to eliminate sharp edges.

3. Cut two Axles, each 4¾ inches long, from the wooden dowel rod.

4. Figure B shows placement of the axle holes in the Base and Wheels. Drill two axle holes through the Base where indicated, using the larger diameter bit. Drill an off-center axle hole through each Wheel, using the smaller bit.

Assembly

1. An assembly diagram for Mama is given in **Figure C.** Begin by attaching the Feet to the Legs, using glue and ¾-inch long nails driven through the bottoms of the Feet and up into the Legs.

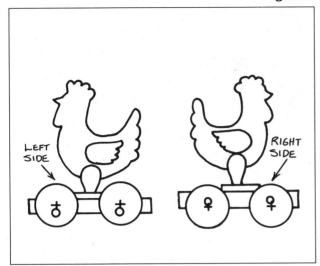

2. Attach the Legs to the Body where indicated in **Figure C**, using glue and the 1-inch long nails. Recess the nails, cover the holes with wood filler, and sand the resulting lumps smooth.

3. Sand the Wings smooth, and glue the Wings to the Body where indicated in **Figure C**.

4. Attach Mama to her Base, centering the Feet between the front, back, and side edges, using glue and ½-inch long nails. Recess the nails, fill the holes with wood filler, and sand the resulting lumps smooth.

5. Insert the Axles through the axle holes in the Base, leaving equal extensions on each side.

6. To achieve the optimum waddle, it is necessary to attach the Wheels correctly. If you will look at one Wheel you will see that, since the axle hole is drilled off-center, there is a larger portion of the Wheel on one side of the hole than on the other. Glue a Wheel to each axle end on the left side of the Base, so that the larger portion of each Wheel is at the top (**Figure D**). Glue the remaining two Wheels to the axle ends on the right side of the Base, so that the larger portion of each Wheel is at the bottom. (Be sure that the axles do not spin, changing the positions of the left-hand Wheels, when you turn the assembly around to attach the right-hand Wheels.) The outer sides of the Wheels should be flush with the axle ends, leaving a short gap between the Base and each Wheel.

CHICKS

Cutting the pieces

1. Full-size patterns for the pieces required to build the chicks are given in **Figure E**. Make a kraft paper pattern for each piece.

2. Cut three Bases, each 2 x 3 inches, and three Bodies from the pine 1 x 8. Cut six each of the Feet, Wings, and Legs from the lattice. Cut twelve Wheels, each 1¼-inches in diameter, from the ½-inch thick lumber. Sand the pieces, eliminating all sharp edges.

3. Cut six Axles, each 3½ inches long, from the wooden dowel rod.

4. Drill two axle holes through each Base, using the larger diameter bit. Placement of the holes is shown in **Figure F**. Use the smaller diameter bit to drill an axle hole ⅜-inch off center, through each Wheel.

Figure F

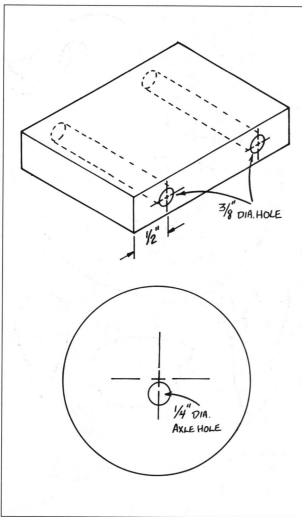

3/8" DIA. HOLE

1/2"

1/4" DIA. AXLE HOLE

Figure G

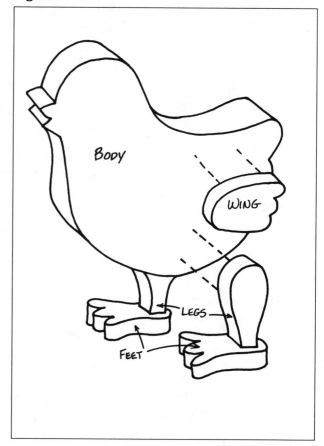

BODY

WING

LEGS

FEET

Assembly

An assembly diagram for the chicks is given in **Figure G**. Follow the assembly instructions for Mama as you build the chicks, with a few minor changes. Do not attempt to use nails when attaching the Feet to the Legs, as the ends of the Legs are extremely small and may split if you drive nails into them. Use the remaining smallest nails to attach the Feet to the Bases, and the Wings to the Bodies. As you attach the Wheels, be sure to follow carefully the instructions given for the Mama's Wheels (see **Figure D**).

Finishing

1. You may wish to connect the chicken family with lengths of cord so that they can be pulled along in a row. If so, you'll need to drill holes in the Bases to accommodate the cotton cord. Use the smaller bit to drill a hole near the front and rear edges of each Base, taking care to avoid drilling into the Axles. (For the chick which will be at the end of the line, drill only the hole near the front edge of the Base.) Cut three 12-inch lengths of cord, and use them to tie the Bases together. Tie the remaining length of cord to the hole near the front edge of the Mama's Base, and use it to pull the entire crew along.

2. Paint or stain your chicken family, and add facial features with paint or felt tip markers when the base coat has dried completely.

Oil Well Pump Jack

Strike it rich in the oil patch! This hand-cranked model has a realistic pumping action and runs on elbow grease to save energy. Overall dimensions are 10 x 24 x 28 inches.

Figure A

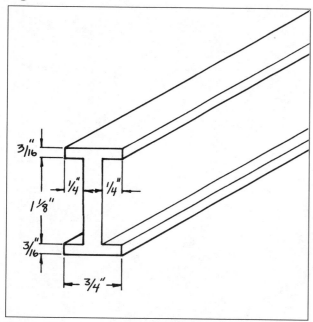

Figure B

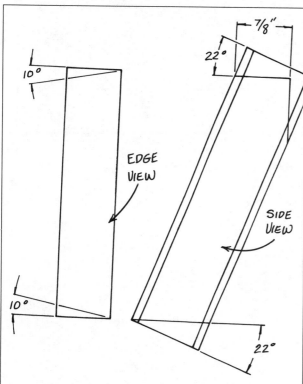

EDGE VIEW

SIDE VIEW

10°

22°

7/8"

22°

10°

22°

Materials

16 linear feet of pine 1 x 2
3 x 3 foot piece of ½ inch interior plywood
11 linear inches of 2 x 6
5 linear inches of ⅛-inch-diameter wooden dowel rod
18 linear inches of 3/16-inch-diameter wooden dowel
6 linear inches of ¼-inch-diameter wooden dowel rod
2 linear inches of ⅜-inch-diameter wooden dowel rod
2 linear inches of ½-inch-diameter wooden dowel rod
3 linear inches of 1-inch-diameter wooden dowel rod
⅜-inch length of 1¼-inch-diameter wooden closet rod
25-inch length of string
No. 18 wire brads, 1 inch long
Two No. 6 gauge flathead wood screws, each 1½ inches long
Carpenter's wood glue and stain or non-toxic paints
(We used blue and red.)

Cutting the Pieces

1. The Rocker Beam, Supports, and Frame pieces
(A, B, C, and D pieces) are cut from 1 x 2, then grooved
to look like steel I-beams, as shown in **Figure A**. For
the Rocker Beam, cut a 17½-inch length of 1 x 2. Cut
a 1⅛-inch-wide groove, ¼ inch deep from end to end
along each side of the beam, centered 3/16 inch from
both edges (**Figure A**). We used a table saw to cut two
narrow grooves along both sides of the piece, then we
moved the saw blade over by ⅛-inch increments and
made repeated passes along both sides to widen them.

2. For the B Supports and C and D Frame pieces, rip
approximately 9 feet of 1 x 2 down to a 1¼-inch width.
In the same manner as you did in step 1, cut a ⅞-inch-
wide I-beam groove, ¼ inch deep in this stock, then cut
the lengths listed here.

Code	Quantity	Length
B	4	11¼ inches
C	2	19 inches
D	3	5 inches

3. The B Supports must be mitered and beveled on
both ends, as shown in **Figure B**. To begin, miter one
end of each Support at a 22-degree angle, as shown in
the side view drawing (**Figure B**). Miter the opposite

Figure C

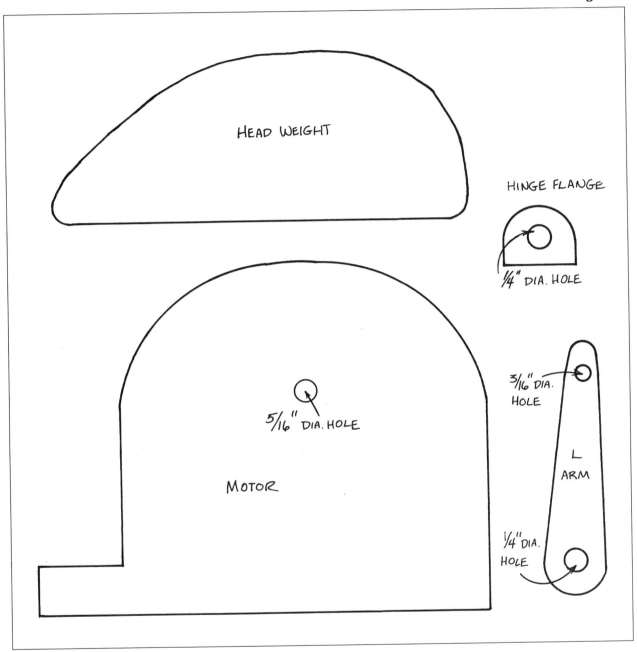

HEAD WEIGHT

HINGE FLANGE

¼" DIA. HOLE

5/16" DIA. HOLE

3/16" DIA. HOLE

MOTOR

L ARM

¼" DIA. HOLE

end at the same angle. Cut one adjacent edge at a 90-degree angle, ⅞ inch from the corner, as shown. On one B Support, bevel both mitered ends at a 10-degree angle, as shown in the edge view (**Figure B**). Bevel

both ends of another B Support at the same angle, making it a mirror image of the first one. Bevel the remaining B Supports in the same manner.

4. A full-size pattern for the rocker beam Head

Figure D

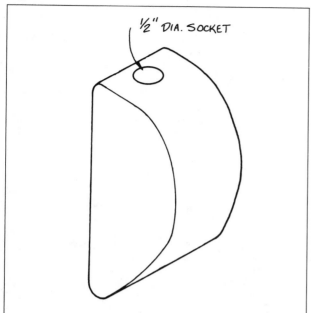

½" DIA. SOCKET

Figure E

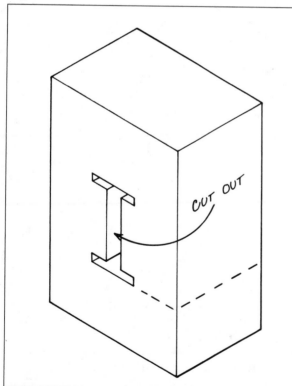

CUT OUT

Figure F

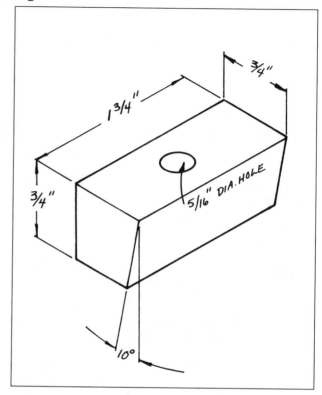

1 ¾"

¾"

¾"

5/16" DIA. HOLE

10°

Weight (E piece) is provided in **Figure C**. Transfer the pattern to a piece of 2 x 6 and cut the Weight. Drill a ½-inch-diameter socket, ¼ inch deep into the upper tip of the curved edge, as shown in **Figure D**. Cut a ½-inch length of ½-inch-diameter dowel to serve as the Cable Pin.

5. Cut a 2¼ x 3½-inch piece of 2 x 6 to serve as the rocker beam Tail Weight. To cut the I-beam slot in the Tail Weight (**Figure E**), position one end of the rocker beam against the wide edge of the Weight, and trace a line around it. Cut the slot using a band or coping saw.

6. The rocker beam pivot assembly consists of two Support Blocks (F pieces), and an Axle Block (G piece). For these pieces, rip a ¾-inch-wide strip from 1 x 2, approximately 8 inches long. From the strip, cut two Support Blocks, each 1¾ inches long, and one Axle Block, 1⅜ inches long. Bevel one long edge of each Support Block at a 10-degree angle, as shown in **Figure F**. In addition, drill a 5/16-inch-diameter socket, ⅜ inch deep into the adjacent long edge, as shown.

THE GREAT MECHANICAL WOODEN TOY BOOK

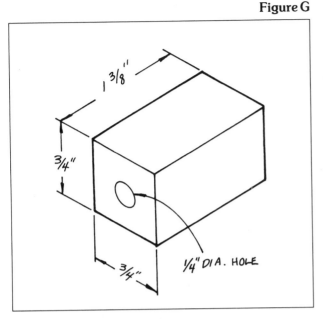

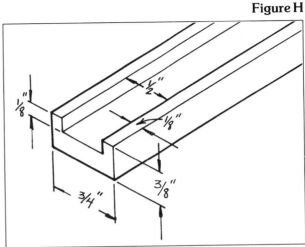

Drill a ¼-inch-diameter hole through the Axle block, as shown in **Figure G**.

7. The drive assembly consists of two short I-beams (H pieces) connected by a cross brace (K piece) between the rocker beam and a pair of motor arms (**Figure Q**). For these pieces, rip a ⅜-inch-wide strip, approximately 3 feet long from 1 x 2. Cut the I-beam motor support pieces (I and J pieces) and Motor Arms (L pieces) from the same strip. To begin, cut a 28-inch length from the strip, and cut a ⅛ x ½-inch groove along one wide edge, as shown in **Figure H**. From the grooved strip, cut the pieces listed here.

Code	Quantity	Length
H	2	7½ inches
I	2	4¾ inches
J	2	1⅞ inches

From the remaining ungrooved strip, cut the pieces listed here. A full-size pattern for the L Arm pieces is provided in **Figure C**.

Code	Quantity	Length
K	1	4 inches
L	2	2¾ inches

Drill a ¼-inch-diameter hole through each L Motor Arm, ⅜ inch from the wider end, as indicated on the pattern (**Figure C**). Drill a ³⁄₁₆-inch-diameter hole ⅜ inch from the opposite end of each Arm, as indicated.

8. A wooden hinge connects the rocker beam to the drive assembly. To begin, rip a ⅛-inch-wide strip approximately 20 inches long from 1 x 2. To save more ripping later, you can cut braces for the rocker beam support and drive assembly from this strip as well as the hinge pieces. A full-size pattern for the hinge Flange (M piece) is provided in **Figure C**. Transfer the pattern to the strip and cut three Flanges. Drill a ¼-inch-diameter hole through each Flange, as indicated on the pattern (**Figure C**). Save the remainder of the strip for later use. Cut a 1½-inch-long Hinge Pin from ³⁄₁₆-inch-diameter dowel, and drill a ⅛-inch-diameter hole through the pin ¼ inch from each end.

9. For braces on the rocker beam support and drive mechanism, use the remainder of the strip you cut in step 8. From the strip, cut two Support Braces (N pieces), each 3½ inches long, and one Drive Brace (O piece), 4¼ inches long. Miter each end of both N Support Braces at a 10-degree angle (**Figure I**).

10. A full-size pattern for the Motor (P piece) is provided in **Figure C**. Transfer the pattern to the remaining length of 2 x 6 and cut one Motor. Drill a ⁵⁄₁₆-inch-diameter hole through the Motor, 2¼ inches from the lower edge, as indicated on the pattern (**Figure C**). In addition, cut one 3-inch length of ¼-inch-diameter dowel

Figure I

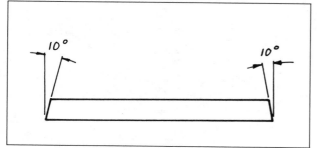

Figure J

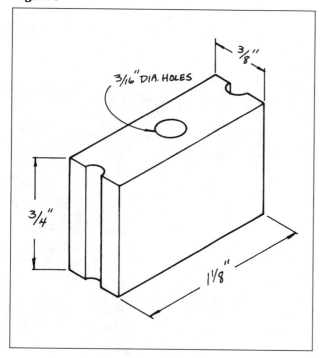

Figure K

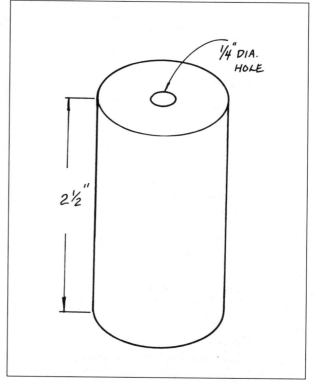

rod to serve as the Motor Hub, two 1-inch lengths of ³⁄₁₆-inch-diameter dowel (Motor Arm and Hinge Pins), and one 2-inch length of ³⁄₈-inch-diameter dowel (crank Handle) for the drive mechanism. Drill a ¹⁄₈-inch-diameter hole through the Hinge Pin, ¹⁄₈ inch from each end.

11. The sucker rod assembly (**Figure U**) consists of a Sucker Rod (Q piece), Cable Clamp (R piece), two Well Caps (S and T pieces), and a Stop piece. For the Q Sucker Rod, cut a 13-inch length of ³⁄₁₆-inch-diameter dowel rod. For the R Cable Clamp, cut a ¾ x ³⁄₈ x 1¹⁄₈-inch piece from 1 x 2. Drill a ³⁄₁₆-inch-diameter

hole through the Clamp, and cut a shallow groove along each narrow edge, as shown in **Figure J**. For the S Well Cap, cut a 2½-inch length of 1-inch-diameter dowel rod, and drill a ¼-inch-diameter hole through the length, as shown in **Figure K**. For the T Well Cap, cut a ³⁄₈-inch-length of 1¼-inch-diameter closet rod, and drill it in the same manner. Cut a ¼-inch length of ½-inch-diameter dowel for the Stop. Drill a ³⁄₁₆-inch-diameter hole through the Stop.

12. For the base, cut the pieces listed here from ½-inch plywood.

Code	Quantity	Dimensions
U	1	10 x 28 inches
V	2	6 x 28 inches
W	2	6 x 9 inches
X	2	4 x 10 inches

Assembly

1. The assembled base is shown in **Figure L**. All

Figure L

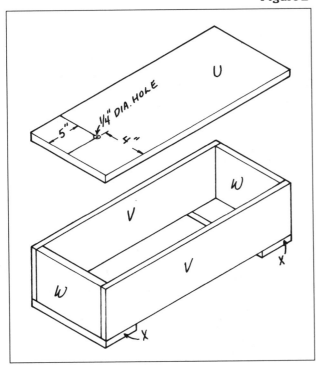

joints are secured using glue and brads. To begin, assemble the V Sides and W Ends, butting the edges as shown with all pieces flush at the lower edge. The edges of the Ends should be covered by the Sides. Attach the U piece to the top of the box, and the X pieces to the bottom, as shown. Drill a ¼-inch-diameter hole through the U Top, 5 inches from the sides and 4 inches from one end, as shown.

2. The frame assembly is shown in **Figure M**. All joints are secured using glue and brads. To begin, install one C piece 1¾ inches from one side of the base, 5⅜ inches from the drilled end, as shown. Install one D piece 1 inch from each end of the C piece, as shown. Install the remaining D piece 3¼ inches from one of the D pieces as shown. Install the remaining C piece, butting it against the D pieces, and lining up the ends with the opposite C piece, as shown. Install one B piece 2 inches from the end of one C piece, so that it tilts in toward the center of the base, as shown. Install another B piece, butting the upper end against the opposite B piece, as shown. Install the two remaining B pieces in the same manner on the opposite C piece, as shown.

Figure M

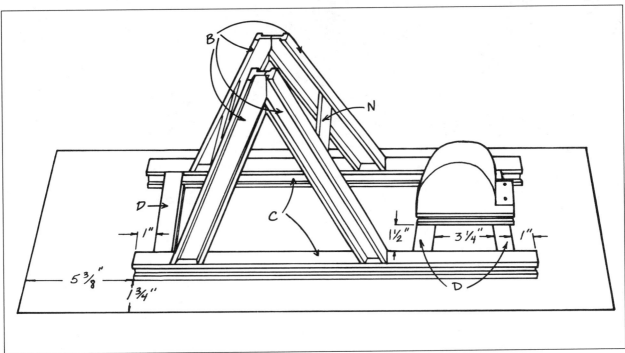

Figure N

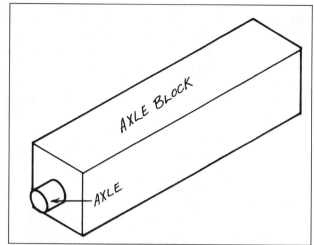

Figure O

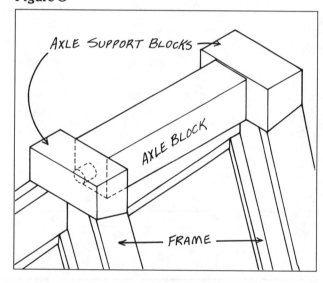

Figure P

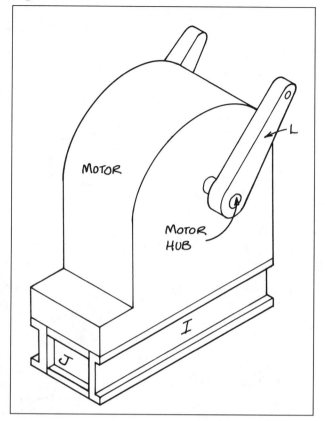

Install one N Support Brace between each pair of B pieces, butting the mitered ends against the B pieces.

3. Glue the Axle in the G Axle Block, so that ¼ inch extends from each end, as shown in **Figure N**. Lubricate each end of the Axle with beeswax.

4. Attach one F Axle Support Block on top of one side of the frame assembly, as shown in **Figure O**. Insert one end of the Axle into the socket in the Support Block, then slide the remaining Support Block over the opposite end of the Axle. Secure the Support Block on top of the opposite side of the frame, as shown.

5. The assembled motor is shown in **Figure P**. To begin, attach the I and J I-beam pieces to the lower edge of the P Motor piece, butting the edges as shown. The ends of the J pieces should be covered by the I pieces, and all pieces should be even with the outer edges of the Motor piece. Lubricate the Motor Hub piece with beeswax, then insert it into the hole in the center of the Motor. Install an L Motor Arm on each end of the Hub, so that both arms are rotated to the same position, as shown in **Figure P**. Install the assembled motor on top of the D pieces, centered between the C pieces, as shown in **Figure M**.

6. The drive assembly is shown in **Figure Q**. To begin, attach the undrilled end of an H piece to each end of the K piece, butting the edges as shown. The K piece should cover the ends of the H pieces. Be sure the grooved edge of each H piece is facing away from the center of the assembly, as shown. Use glue and

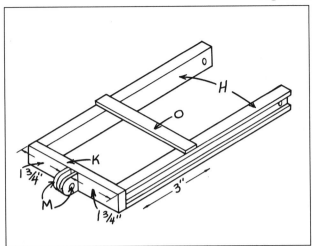

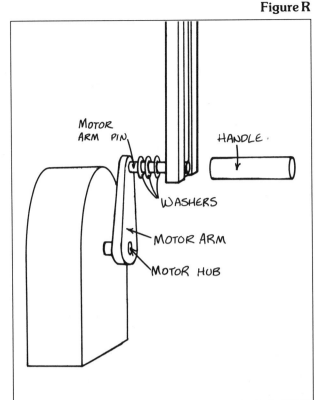

screws to attach the **O** piece between the two **H** pieces, 3 inches from the upper end, as shown. Attach two **M** Hinge pieces, each 1¾ inches from the end of the **K** piece, as shown.

7. To attach the drive assembly to the Motor Arms, slip one Motor Arm Pin through the hole in one **H** piece, as shown in **Figure R**. Slip three washers over the end of the pin, then insert it into the hole in the Motor Arm, as shown. Repeat this procedure to attach the opposite side of the drive assembly. On one side, slip the drilled end of the Handle over the Motor Arm Pin, as shown.

8. Attach the Head and Tail Weights to the **A** Rocker Beam, as shown in **Figure S**. To attach the Head Weight, we drilled a starter hole at an angle through the top and bottom of the Beam, then inserted brads. Glue the Cable Pin in the socket in the Head Weight. Slide the Tail Weight along the Beam, and glue it ¾ inch from the end. Glue the remaining **M** Hinge piece to the underside of the Beam, 2 inches from the Tail Weight.

9. To install the Rocker Beam, attach it to the pivot assembly, 6⅝ inches from the Head Weight, as shown in **Figure T**. Insert brads through the lower edge of the Beam into the Axle Block. To attach the drive assembly to the Hinge on the Rocker Beam, align the holes in all three Hinge pieces, and insert the drilled Hinge Pin, as shown in **Figure T**. Insert a length of ⅛-inch-diameter dowel in each hole in the Hinge Pin to secure it.

10. The sucker rod assembly is shown in **Figure U**. To begin, slide the **R** piece down the **Q** piece, and glue

Figure S

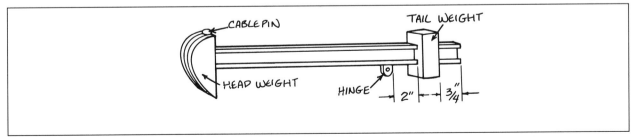

Figure T

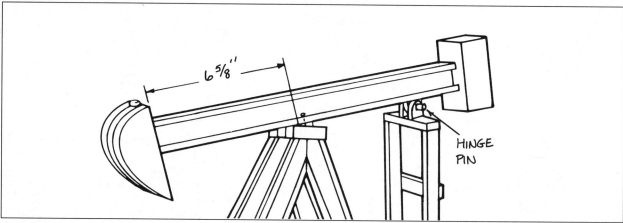

6⅝"

HINGE PIN

Figure U

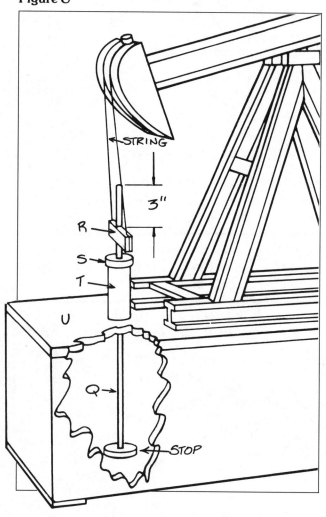

STRING

3"

R

S

T

U

Q

STOP

it in place 3 inches from one end, as shown. Align the holes in the S and T pieces, and glue them together. Glue the assembled well cap to the U Base piece, aligning the holes as shown. Slide the end of the sucker rod into the hole in the well cap, as shown. Inside the base, glue the Stop piece over the end of the rod, as shown. Tie a knot in one end of the string and press the string into the groove in one edge of the R piece, as shown. With the Head Weight in its highest position, and the sucker rod pulled up as far as it will go, wrap the string around the dowel rod piece at the upper end of the Head Weight and glue in place. Press the free end of the string into the remaining groove on the R piece, and tie a knot below it. Glue the string into the groove, and cut off any excess below the knot.

11. Stain or paint the oil well pump, lubricate the sucker rod with beeswax so it will operate smoothly, then crank 'er up! (If you strike oil, let us know — we'll be glad to help you pump it out!) We painted the base and rocker beam weights red, and the frame blue. For an all–American (or should we say Texican?) touch, we added red, white, and blue stick-on stars to accent the rocker beam and supports.

12. To create an authentic oil-patch gravel bed, spread glue over the surface of the base, and sprinkle on aquarium gravel. (Don't worry, it won't contaminate your crude.) We don't recommend this last step if the pump jack will be within reach of small children or rock eating pets.

THE GREAT MECHANICAL WOODEN TOY BOOK

Biplane

De plane! De plane! Suitable for dogfights, crop dusting, or flights of fancy, this vintage biplane features a hidden mechanism that spins the propeller as the plane rolls along the runway. Overall dimensions are 8 x 12 x 13 inches.

Materials

8 linear feet of ½ x 3½-inch pine (Pine of this thickness is manufactured in different widths, so the length of the piece you'll need will depend on the width available. You'll need a piece at least 3½ inches wide.)

4 linear inches of pine 2 x 4

4¼-inch length of ¼-inch-diameter wooden dowel rod

2-foot length of ⅜-inch-diameter wooden dowel rod

¼-inch length of ¾-inch-diameter wooden dowel rod

No. 6 flathead wood screws: three ¾ inch long, five 1 inch long, and two 1½ inches long

Pilot (Most hobby shops carry a variety of little dowel people, or you can make a pilot from a ¾-inch-diameter spherical wooden drawer pull and a 1½-inch length of ¾-inch-diameter wooden dowel rod.)

Carpenter's wood glue

Two heavy-duty rubber bands, each 2½ inches long

Cutting the Pieces

1. Scale drawings for the biplane parts are provided in **Figure C**. Enlarge the drawings to make full-size patterns. Use the patterns to cut the pieces from the materials specified below.

Description	Quantity	Material
Propeller	1	½-inch pine
Nose Cone	1	2 x 4
Wheel	2	½-inch pine
Wheel Support	3	½-inch pine
Upper Wing	1	½-inch pine
Lower Wing	1	½-inch pine
Body	3	½-inch pine
Horizontal Tail	1	½-inch pine
Vertical Tail	1	½-inch pine

2. Two Body pieces form the outer layers of the assembled biplane body, and each one must be contoured on one side. Cut the contours on one Body as shown in the Top View drawing in **Figure C**. Cut the contours on another Body, making it a mirror image of the first piece.

3. The remaining uncontoured Body must be notched and drilled to accommodate the propeller mechanism. Drill a ¼-inch-diameter socket 2½ inches deep into the front end of the remaining Body, ⅞ inch

Figure A

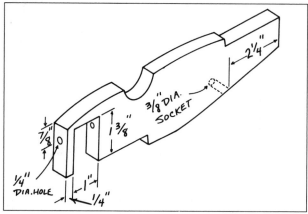

Figure B

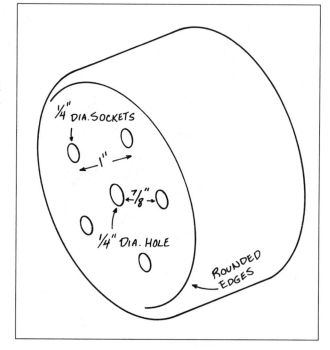

from the upper edge, as shown in **Figure A**. In addition, cut a 1 x 1⅜-inch notch into the lower edge of this piece ¼ inch from the front end, as shown. For the rear skid, drill a ⅜-inch-diameter socket, at a 15-degree angle and ⅜ inch deep, into the lower edge of this Body, 2¼ inches from the rear end, as shown.

4. Drill a ¼-inch-diameter hole through the Propeller where indicated on the scale drawing in **Figure C**. For

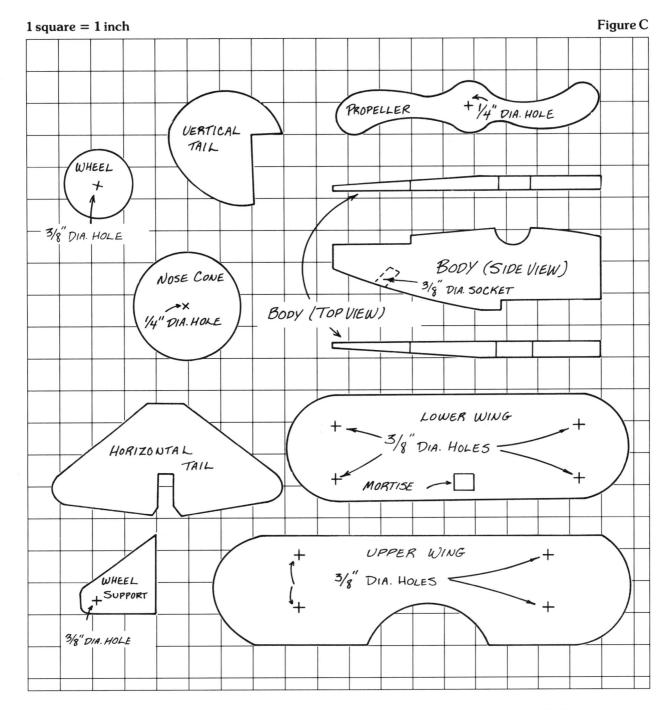

the Propeller Shaft, drill a ¼-inch-diameter hole through the exact center of the Nose Cone. Drill five ¼-inch-diameter sockets 1 inch deep into the front side of

the Nose Cone, spacing them evenly ⅞ inch from the center hole, as shown in **Figure B**. In addition, enlarge the center hole on the opposite (rear) side of the Nose

Figure D

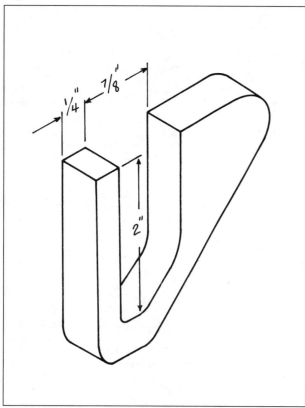

Figure E

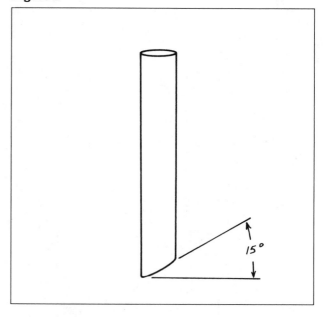

Cone, to create a 1-inch-diameter recess, ⅜ inch deep. A wooden washer housed in the recess keeps the Propeller Shaft from slipping out of the Nose Cone. To create the washer, drill a ¼-inch-diameter hole through the length of the ¾-inch-diameter wooden dowel rod. Round off the circumference of the front side of the Nose Cone, as shown.

5. Drill a ⅜-inch-diameter axle hole through each Wheel Support, where indicated on the scale drawing in **Figure C**. One Wheel Support must be notched to accommodate the rubber band that drives the propeller shaft. Cut the notch in one Wheel Support, where indicated in **Figure D**. Drill a ⅜-inch-diameter axle hole through the exact center of each Wheel.

6. Drill ⅜-inch-diameter holes through the Upper and Lower Wings where indicated on the scale drawings in **Figure C**. Cut a ½-inch square mortise through the Lower Wing, ¼ inch from one long edge.

7. Cut the pieces listed here from the specified sizes of wooden dowel rod.

Description	Quantity	Length	Dowel
Skid	1	2⅜ inches	⅜-inch
Axle	1	2¾ inches	⅜-inch
Wing Support	4	4⅜ inches	⅜-inch
Propeller Shaft	1	4½ inches	¼-inch

8. Miter one end of the Skid at a 15-degree angle, as shown in **Figure E**.

Assembly

Note: Do not use glue on any joints unless instructed to do so.

1. Assemble the three Body pieces by inserting two 1-inch screws through each contoured outer Body into the inner Body, 1¾ inches from the front end, as shown in **Figure F**. Countersink the screws. For the pilot, drill a ¾-inch-diameter socket ⅝ inch deep, into the upper edge of the assembled body, at the base of the cockpit contour, as shown. Note: if you purchased a pre-made pilot of a different size, drill the socket to accommodate the pilot.

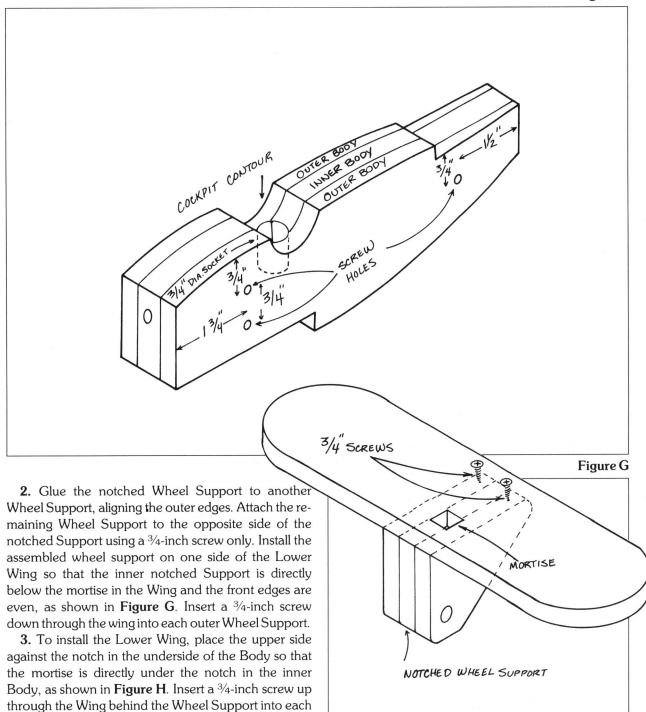

Figure G

2. Glue the notched Wheel Support to another Wheel Support, aligning the outer edges. Attach the remaining Wheel Support to the opposite side of the notched Support using a ¾-inch screw only. Install the assembled wheel support on one side of the Lower Wing so that the inner notched Support is directly below the mortise in the Wing and the front edges are even, as shown in **Figure G**. Insert a ¾-inch screw down through the wing into each outer Wheel Support.

3. To install the Lower Wing, place the upper side against the notch in the underside of the Body so that the mortise is directly under the notch in the inner Body, as shown in **Figure H**. Insert a ¾-inch screw up through the Wing behind the Wheel Support into each outer Body piece.

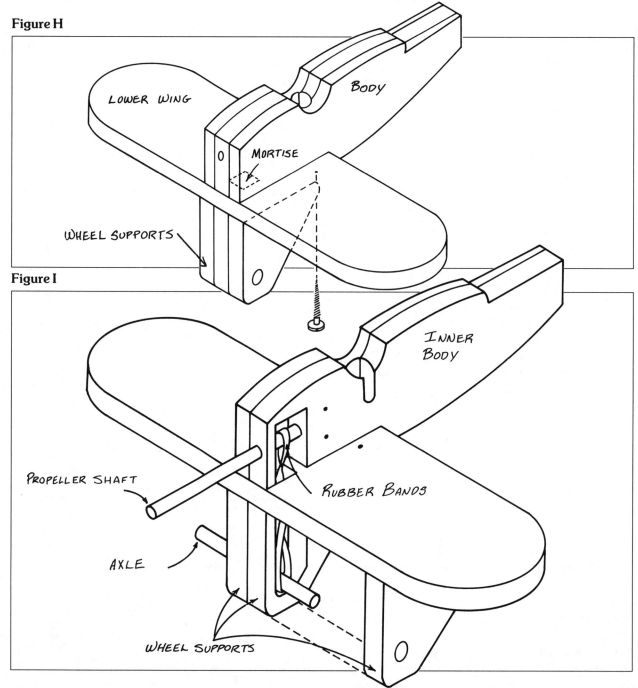

LOWER WING

BODY

MORTISE

0

WHEEL SUPPORTS

Figure I

INNER
BODY

PROPELLER SHAFT

RUBBER BANDS

AXLE

WHEEL SUPPORTS

4. To assemble the propeller mechanism, remove the two body screws and the lower wing screw to remove one outer Body piece, as shown in **Figure I**. In addition, remove the outer Wheel Support on the same side of the biplane, as shown. Thread two rubber bands together through the mortise in the Lower Wing, leaving equal loops on each end. Insert one end of the Propeller Shaft through the hole in the front end of the body, slip it through the rubber band loops, and push it into the socket on the opposite side of the notch, as shown. Insert one end of the Axle through the hole in one Wheel Support, and slip it through the rubber band loops, as shown. Since the Propeller Shaft and the Axle are perpendicular to each other, the rubber bands will have a twist in the middle. Re-install the Wheel Support and outer Body piece you removed earlier.

5. To install one Wheel, slip it over one end of the Axle and glue it in place, flush with the outer end of the Axle. Install the remaining Wheel on the opposite end of the Axle in the same manner.

6. Slip the wooden washer over the end of the Propeller Shaft, and slide it down the Shaft until it is $1/16$ inch from the front end of the body. Glue the washer to the Shaft, but be careful not to glue it to the body.

7. To install the Nose Cone, slip the center hole over the Propeller Shaft and slide it down the shaft until the rear side is against the front end of the body, as shown in **Figure J**. Rotate the Nose Cone until one socket is aligned with the outer Body piece on each side, as shown. Insert a $1\frac{1}{2}$-inch screw into each aligned socket and screw it into the front end of the body.

8. To install the Propeller, slip the center hole over the end of the Propeller Shaft. Glue it in place, flush with the end of the Shaft, being careful to avoid glueing the Propeller to the Nose Cone.

9. To install the Upper Wing, insert one end of a Wing Support into each hole in the Lower Wing and glue in place. The lower ends of the Supports should be flush with the underside of the Lower Wing. Slip the Upper Wing over the opposite ends of the Supports and glue in place. Be sure to turn the Upper Wing so that the contoured edge is facing toward the rear.

10. To install the Horizontal Tail, place one side against the notch in the upper edge of the body, as shown in **Figure K**. Insert two 1-inch screws down through the Tail into the inner Body piece. To install the Vertical Tail, slip the extension at the back of the notch into the notch in the rear of the Horizontal Tail, as shown. Glue the Vertical Tail to the Horizontal Tail.

11. To install the Skid, insert the unmitered end into the socket in the underside of the body. Rotate the Skid until the mitered end rests flat on the floor, and glue.

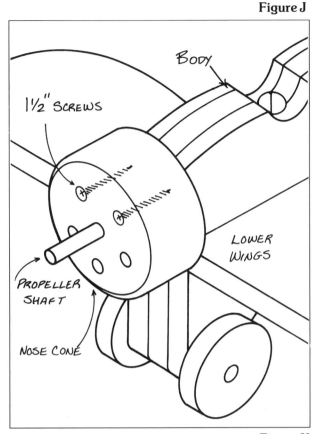

Figure J

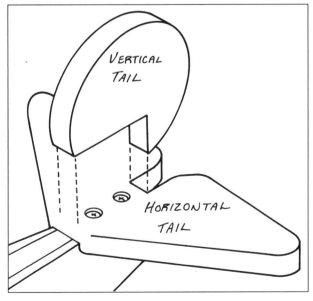

Figure K

Cog Machine

The ultimate mechanical wooden toy! In these modern times, everybody needs a great do-nothing contraption like this to crank up drooping spirits and keep the wheels of industry turning. Overall dimensions are 8 x 17 x 19 inches.

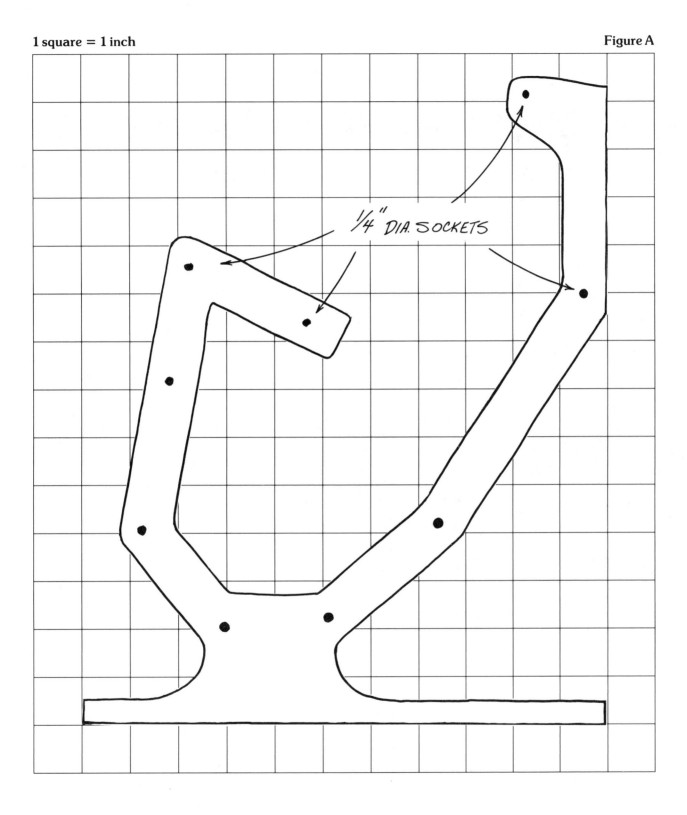

¼" DIA. SOCKETS

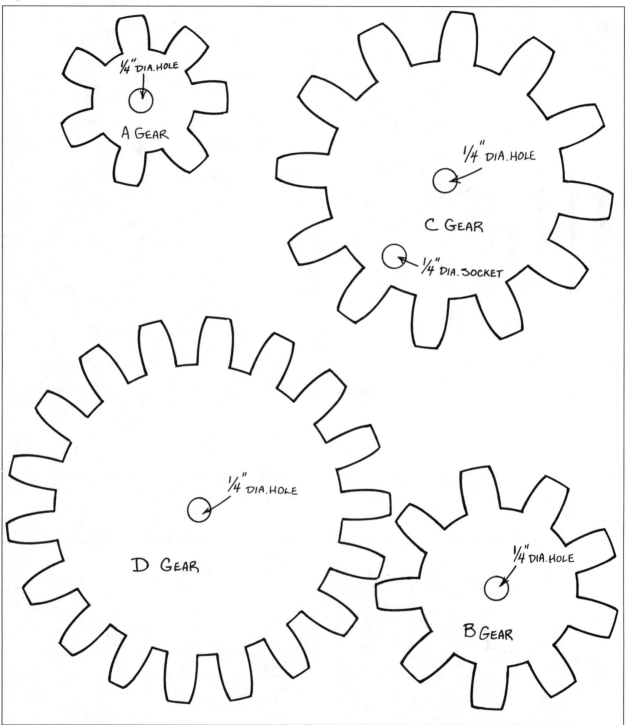

Magical Motion Machine – page 20

Chirpin' Chicks – page 30

Oil Well Pump Jack – page 35

Biplane – page 45

Cog Machine – page 52

Eye-catcher Eagle Whirligig – page 59

Fantastic Freight Train – page 68

Fantastic Freight Train – page 68

Whirling Ferris Wheel – page 92

Spinning Carousel – page 105

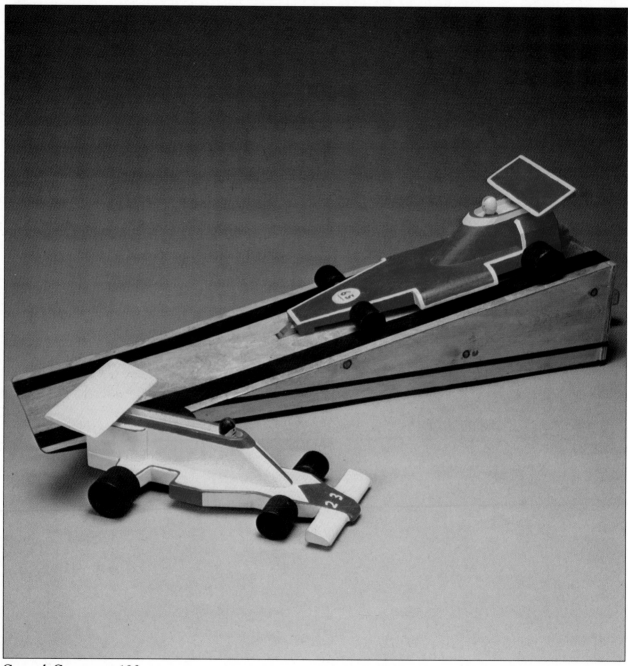

Catapult Cars – page 120

Figure C

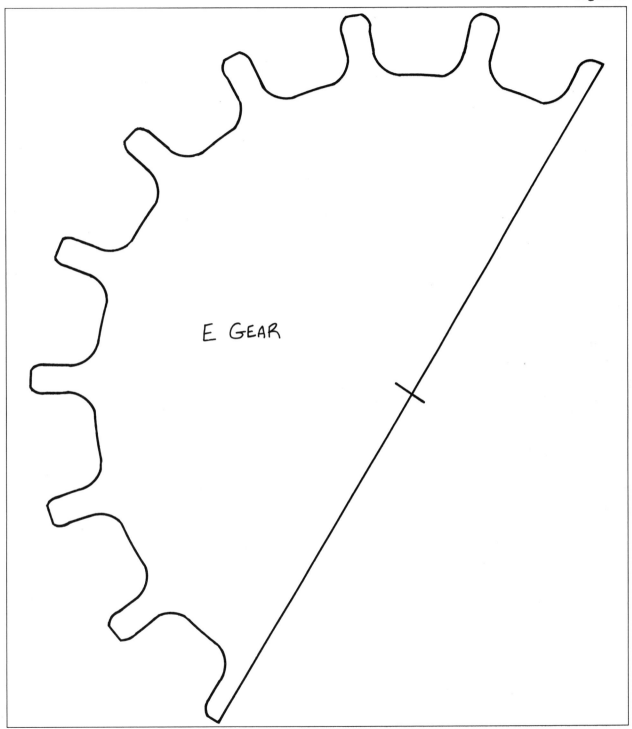

E GEAR

Figure D

¼" DIA. HOLE

Materials

2-foot square of ¾-inch veneer core plywood
8-inch square of ½-inch plywood
¼-inch-diameter wooden pegs: nine 1¼ inches long,
and one 3¼ inches long

¼-inch length of ⅜-inch-diameter wooden dowel rod
2½-inch length of ½-inch-diameter wooden dowel rod
Paint in your choice of colors (we used blue, green, yellow, red, orange, purple, brown, and white).

Cutting the Pieces

After you've cut these pieces, the assembly is as easy as falling off a "cog," so take your time while you're cutting the gears.

1. For the Base, cut an 8 x 11-inch piece from ¾-inch plywood. Cut a ¾-inch-wide groove ½ inch deep along one side of the Base, from end to end and centered between the two long edges.

2. A scale drawing for the Gear Support is provided in **Figure A**. Enlarge the drawing to make a full-size paper pattern and cut one Gear Support from ¾-inch plywood. Drill ¼-inch-diameter sockets ¼ inch deep into one side of the Support where indicated.

3. Full-size patterns for the smaller gears are provided in **Figure B**. Trace the patterns, and carefully cut from ¾-inch plywood one A Gear, two B Gears, three C Gears, and one D Gear. A full-size pattern for half of the E Gear is provided in **Figure C**. Trace the pattern twice, tape the halves together to make a complete pattern, and cut one E Gear from ¾-inch plywood. Drill a ¼-inch-diameter hole through the exact center of each gear, as indicated on the patterns. In addition, drill a ¼-inch-diameter socket ½ inch deep into one C Gear, 1 inch from the end of one tooth, as shown in **Figure B**.

4. A full-size pattern for the bucking bronco and rider is provided in **Figure D**. Cut one bronco and rider from ½-inch plywood. Drill a ¼-inch-diameter hole through the bronco where indicated on the pattern. When installed, the bronco will pivot on a wooden peg. A Spacer slipped over the peg keeps the bronco from rubbing against its support. To create the Spacer, drill a ¼-inch-diameter hole through the center length of the ⅜-inch-diameter dowel rod.

5. For the handle Sleeve, drill a ⁵⁄₁₆-inch-diameter hole through the center length of the ½-inch-diameter dowel rod.

Assembly

1. To assemble the support structure, slide the lower edge of the Gear Support into the groove in the Base and glue in place, as shown in **Figure E**.

2. To assemble the handle, slip the 3-inch peg into the handle Sleeve, and insert the peg end into the off-center socket in the C Gear, as shown in **Figure F** Glue

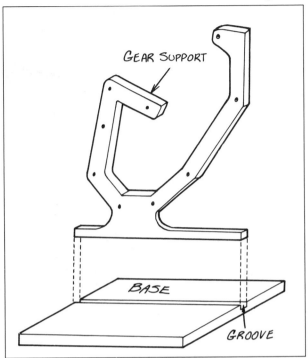

Figure E

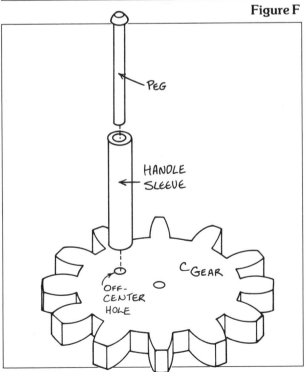

Figure F

Figure G

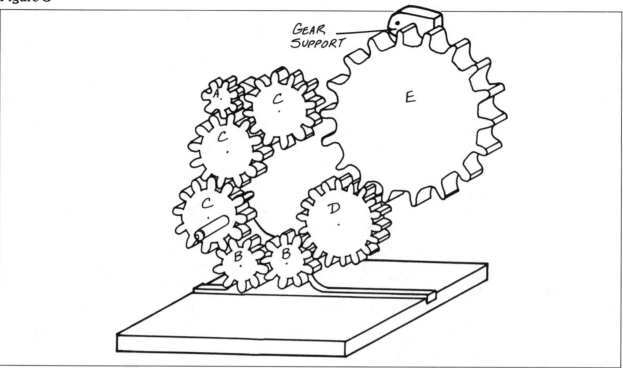

Figure H

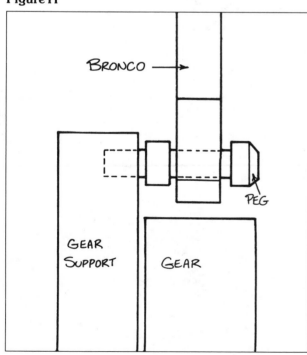

the peg into the socket, but do not glue the Sleeve to the peg.

3. The gears are installed on the Support as shown in **Figure G**. To install one gear, slip a short peg through the center hole and insert the end into a socket in the Support. Glue each gear peg into its socket, leaving the gear loose enough to rotate smoothly.

4. The bucking bronco is pegged to the uppermost hole in the Gear Support, as shown in **Figure H**. Slip a peg through the hole in the bronco, and add the Spacer before you insert the peg end into the socket. Glue the peg into the socket, but be careful not to get any glue on the spacer or bronco.

5. Stain and/or paint the cog machine. We chose to stain the base and support and paint only the surfaces of the gears. This scheme has the obvious advantage of keeping sticky paint out of the gear teeth, but go ahead and throw a wrench in the works if you want to. It's also important not to get any paint in the holes that house the pegs. To make the gears turn more smoothly, rub wax on the teeth.

THE GREAT MECHANICAL WOODEN TOY BOOK

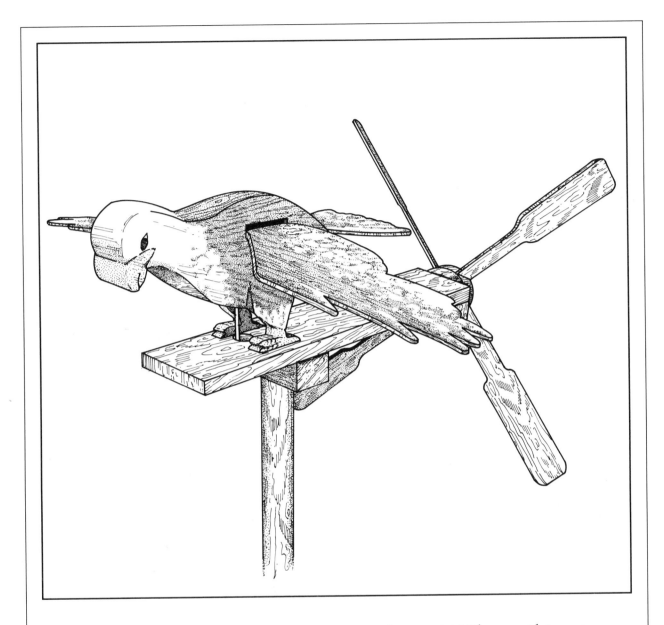

Eye-catcher Eagle Whirligig

This proud bird is 17 inches long, 10 inches tall, and has a wingspan of 26 inches. A shaft mechanism causes his wings to flap when the wind spins the propeller.

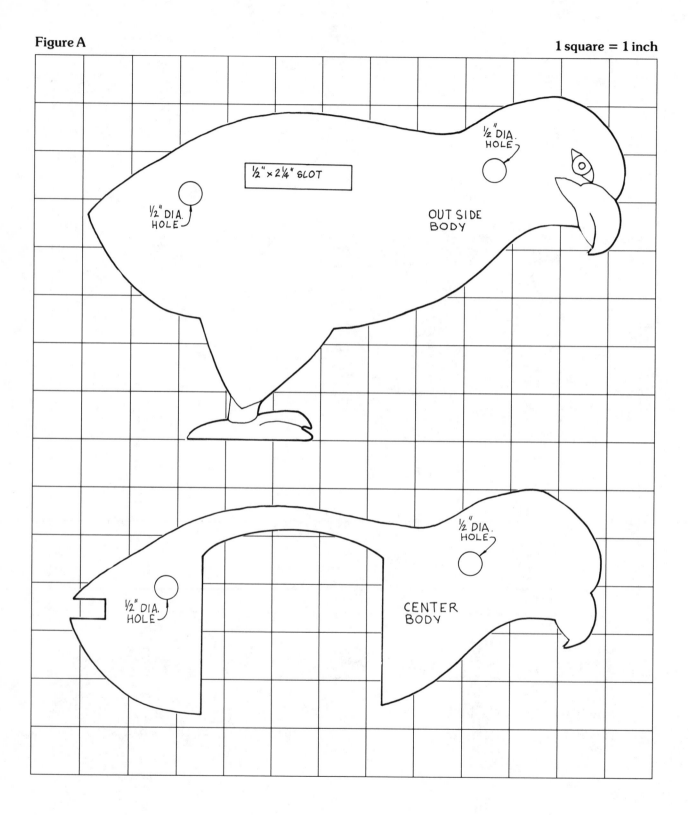

½ "DIA.
HOLE

½ "×2¼" SLOT

½ "DIA.
HOLE

OUT SIDE
BODY

½ "DIA.
HOLE

½ "DIA.
HOLE

CENTER
BODY

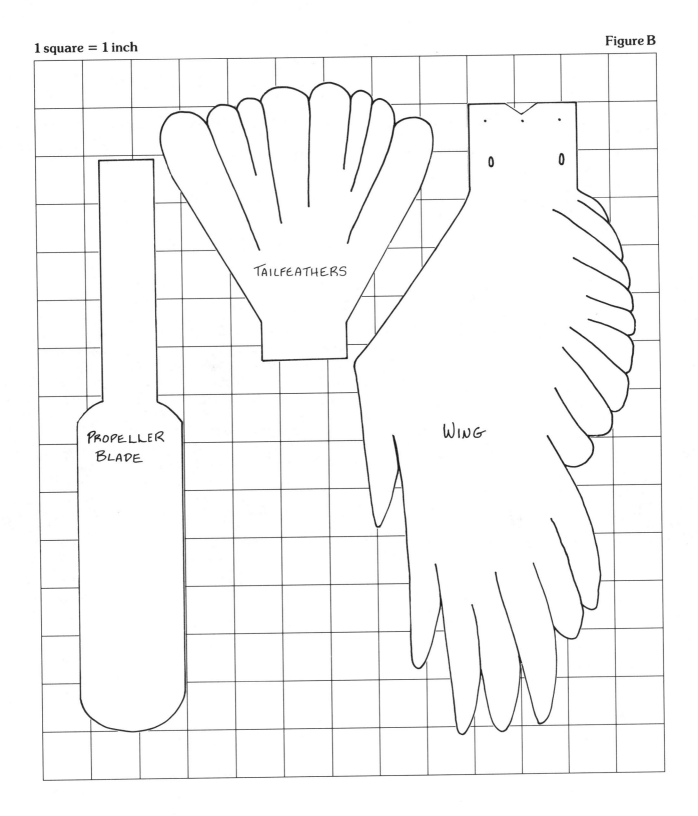

Figure C

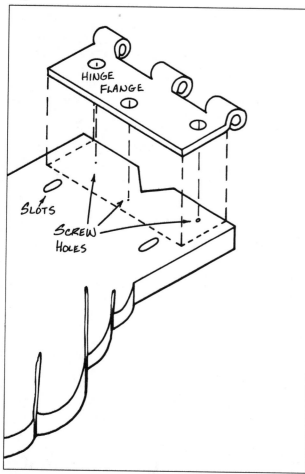

HINGE FLANGE

SLOTS

SCREW HOLES

Materials

13 x 13-inch piece of ⅛-inch exterior grade plywood

14 x 24-inch piece of ¼-inch exterior grade plywood

6 x 12-inch piece of ⁸⁄₄ pine (Eight-quarters lumber is 1¾ inches thick; if a piece near this size is not available, you can glue several thinner boards together.)

5 linear feet of pine 1 x 8

5-inch length of pine 2 x 4

One brass loose-pin hinge, 2 inches long

7½-inch length of ³⁄₁₆-inch-diameter threaded steel rod, with four hex nuts, two lock washers, and two flat washers

5-inch length of ⅜-inch-diameter copper tubing

17½-inch length of ¼-inch-diameter steel rod, with a ⁷⁄₆₄-inch-diameter hole drilled ⅜ inch from one end (Many metal shops or service stations will drill the rod for you.)

One coil spring, approximately ⅜ inch in diameter and 1¼ inches long

No. 6 gauge flathead wood screws, each 2 inches long

4d and 8d finishing nails

Waterproof glue, exterior wood stain and sealer, and small amounts of brown, black, white and yellow exterior paints

Cutting the Pieces

1. The eagle's body consists of a piece of contoured ⁸⁄₄ wood sandwiched between two pieces of 1 x 8. A scale drawing for the Side Body is provided in **Figure A**. Enlarge the drawing and cut one Side Body from 1 x 8. Cut out a ½ x 2¼-inch slot in the Body where indicated. In addition, drill a ½-inch-diameter hole through the Body where indicated on the pattern. Use this Body as a guide to cut, slot, and drill a second one, so they will be identical and the slots and holes will be perfectly aligned.

2. A scale drawing for the Center Body is provided in **Figure A**. Enlarge the drawing, and cut one Center Body from the ⁸⁄₄ pine. Drill ½-inch-diameter holes where indicated.

3. Scale drawings for the Wings and Tailfeathers are provided in **Figure B**. Enlarge the drawings and cut two Wings and one Tailfeathers from ¼-inch plywood. To make the feathers more realistic, cut a narrow groove along each line on the pattern, using a bandsaw or saber saw. Drill two slots through each Wing where indicated on the pattern. In addition, place one flange of the hinge over the slotted end of each Wing, mark the holes, and drill a screw starter socket for each one, as shown in **Figure C**. It's a good idea to stain or paint the Wings and Tailfeathers and allow them to dry before you start the assembly process.

4. For the Base, rip a 20-inch length of 1 x 8 down to 3½ inches wide. Drill a 1½-inch-diameter hole through the Base, centered 4¼ inches from one end, as shown in **Figure D**. In addition, drill a ⅛-inch-diameter hole through the Base 5⅛ inches from the same end and ¾ inch from each long edge, as shown.

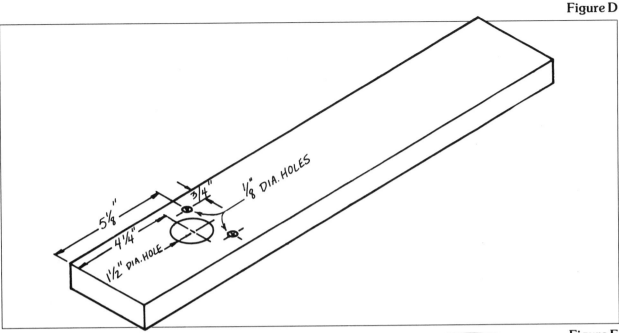

5. A full-size pattern for the Propeller Blade is provided in **Figure B**. Transfer the pattern and cut four Blades from ⅛-inch plywood.

6. For the wing-flapping mechanism, cut a 1½-inch-diameter Cam, and a 3-inch-diameter Hub from 1 x 8. Drill a ¼-inch-diameter hole through the center of each piece. In addition, cut four ⅛-inch-wide notches, each 1 inch deep into the Hub at a 40-degree angle, as shown in **Figure E**. The notches should be evenly spaced around the Hub, as shown. Drill a ⁷⁄₆₄-inch-diameter hole from the outer curved edge of the Hub to the center hole.

7. Cut two lengths of 2 x 4 to serve as the Drive Rod Supports. Cut one Support 2 inches long and the other 3 inches long. Drill a ⅜-inch-diameter hole through each Support, centered ⅜ inch from one long edge, as shown in **Figure F**.

8. Drill a ⅛-inch-diameter hole through the threaded shaft, ⁵⁄₁₆ inch from one end. If you do not have the proper tools, most auto mechanic shops will drill the piece for you. Be sure the hole is large enough to accommodate the shaft of a 4d finishing nail.

Assembly

1. The assembled Body is shown in **Figure G**. To

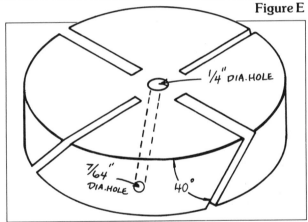

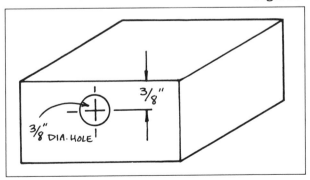

Figure G

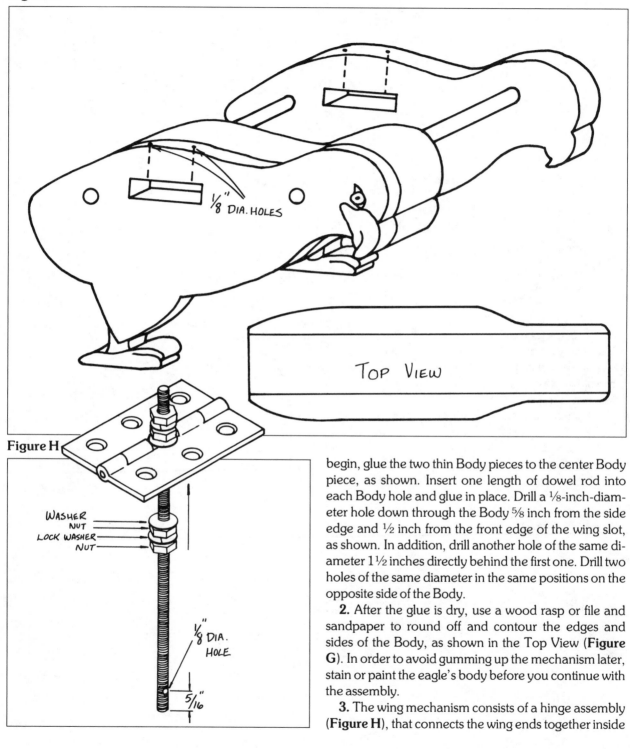

1/8" DIA. HOLES

TOP VIEW

Figure H

WASHER
NUT
LOCK WASHER
NUT

1/8" DIA. HOLE

5/16"

begin, glue the two thin Body pieces to the center Body piece, as shown. Insert one length of dowel rod into each Body hole and glue in place. Drill a 1/8-inch-diameter hole down through the Body 5/8 inch from the side edge and 1/2 inch from the front edge of the wing slot, as shown. In addition, drill another hole of the same diameter 1 1/2 inches directly behind the first one. Drill two holes of the same diameter in the same positions on the opposite side of the Body.

2. After the glue is dry, use a wood rasp or file and sandpaper to round off and contour the edges and sides of the Body, as shown in the Top View (**Figure G**). In order to avoid gumming up the mechanism later, stain or paint the eagle's body before you continue with the assembly.

3. The wing mechanism consists of a hinge assembly (**Figure H**), that connects the wing ends together inside

Figure I

Figure J

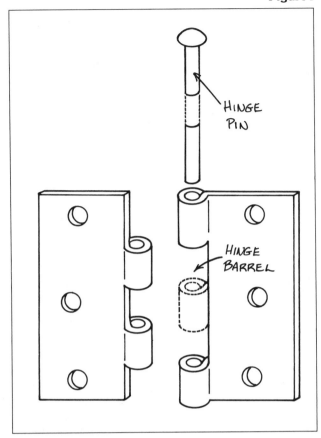

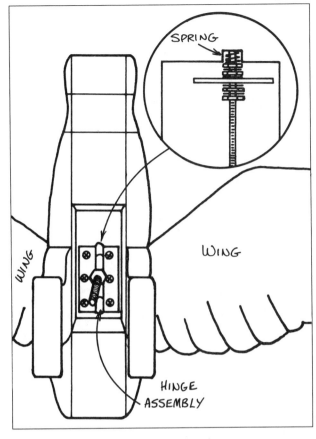

the body cavity, as shown in **Figure J**. To begin, re-move the hinge pin and cut off the center portion of the hinge barrel, as shown in **Figure I**. Cut the hinge pin into two short lengths that will fit in the remaining ends of the barrel and reassemble the hinge. Insert the un-drilled end of the threaded shaft into the opening in the hinge barrel, as shown in **Figure H**. Slip a washer over the shaft end above the hinge, and install a hex nut, a lock washer, and another hex nut, leaving about ½ inch of the shaft extending beyond the nuts. Install a washer, a nut, a lock washer, and another nut on the drilled end of the shaft, and twist the nuts up the shaft until they are about ¼ inch from the hinge.

4. To attach the hinge assembly to the wings, place the Body on its back, as shown in **Figure J**. Drill a ⅜-inch-diameter socket, ¼ inch deep, centered in the un-derside of the body cavity. Insert one end of the coil

spring into the socket. Insert the end of one Wing into each wing slot, as shown (**Figure J**). Hold the hinge as-sembly near the drilled end of the shaft and lower it into the body cavity, aligning the hinge holes with the screw sockets in one Wing, and inserting the shaft end into the spring, as shown. Insert screws through each hinge hole into the sockets on both Wings. Turn the eagle right side up and insert a finishing nail into each hole in the top and down through the Wing slots, to hold the Wings in place as they flap. Test the mechanism – the Wings should flap easily as you pull the threaded shaft up and down. If they don't, try loosening the nuts under the hinge just a bit.

5. The base consists of two Axle Supports with cop-per tubing sleeves that are installed on the Base piece. Cut the copper tubing into one 3-inch length and one 2-inch length. Insert the 3-inch length into the hole in

Figure K

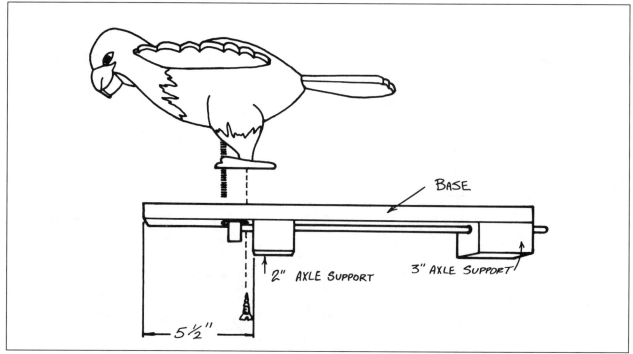

BASE

2" AXLE SUPPORT

3" AXLE SUPPORT

5½"

Figure L

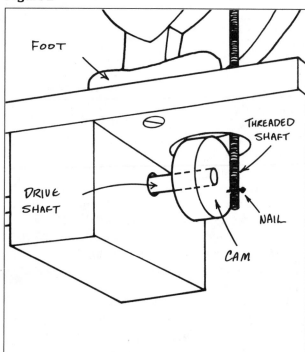

FOOT

THREADED SHAFT

DRIVE SHAFT

NAIL

CAM

the 3-inch Axle Support. Insert the remaining length of tubing into the shorter Support in the same manner. To assemble the base, install the 3-inch Axle Support on the end of the Base piece opposite the hole, as shown in **Figure K**. Install the remaining Axle Support 5½ inches from the hole end, as shown.

6. Install the eagle on the base, using glue and inserting a screw up through the base into each foot, as shown in **Figure L**. The threaded shaft of the wing hinge assembly should extend through the hole in the base, as shown. Insert one end of the Tailfeathers into the slot at the back of the eagle, and glue in place.

7. The threaded shaft of the wing hinge assembly is connected to the Cam, which is mounted on one end of the Drive Shaft, as shown in **Figure L**. To begin, insert a finishing nail approximately ½ inch from the edge of the Cam, leaving ⅜ inch extending above the surface. Insert the Drive Shaft through the Supports, and into the hole in the Cam. Slip the hole in the threaded shaft over the nail in the Cam, as shown.

8. To assemble the Propeller, insert one end of each Propeller Blade into each notch in the Hub, as shown

THE GREAT MECHANICAL WOODEN TOY BOOK

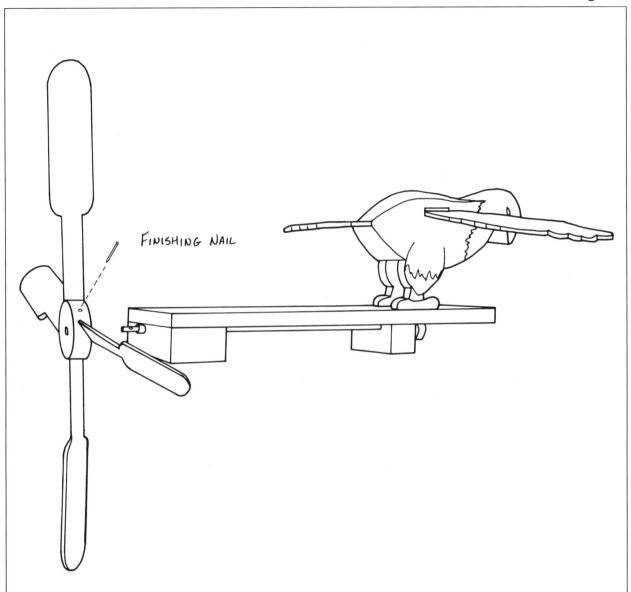

FINISHING NAIL

in **Figure M**, and glue in place. Slip the Hub on the end of the Drive Shaft, so that the holes are aligned. Insert an 8d finishing nail into the Hub edge hole and push it through the Shaft hole to secure the Propeller.

Finishing

1. We stained the whole bird during assembly, then used exterior white paint on his bald head, breast and wing tips. In addition, paint the beak and feet yellow, and outline the eyes with black. Apply an exterior wood sealer over the entire whirligig, being careful not to coat any moving parts.

2. Install the whirligig where it will catch a good, stiff breeze (a high fence post is a good place), and be sure it's secure – or your eagle may head for the hills with the next strong wind.

Fantastic Freight Train

Here's a real railroader's old-time freight train that features a working hopper car, tank car, and crane loader, plus an engine, coal car, flatbed car, and caboose. Your fireman can even stoke the boiler through a trap door in the engine cab. Each of the seven cars is approximately 10 inches long, 7 inches tall, and 3½ inches wide. The tracks can easily be arranged and rearranged in just about any layout.

Materials

8 linear feet of ½ x 3½-inch clear white pine (Pine of this thickness is supplied in different widths, so the length of the piece you'll need will depend upon how wide it is. A width as narrow as 3½ inches will accommodate the pieces you'll need to cut.)

10 linear feet of clear white pine 1 x 6

14 linear inches of pine 2 x 4

2-foot-square piece of ¼-inch plywood, finished on both sides

4-foot-square piece of ¼-inch waferwood for the tracks

10-inch length of ⅛-inch-diameter wooden dowel rod

2-inch length of ³⁄₁₆-inch-diameter wooden dowel rod

4-inch length of ½-inch-diameter wooden dowel rod

3-foot length of ¼-inch-diameter wooden dowel rod

3-inch length of ¾-inch-diameter wooden dowel rod

6-inch length of 1-inch-diameter wooden dowel rod

3-inch length of 2 x 2-inch pine, for turning to create a smokestack (If you don't feel like cranking up the lathe for just one small piece, many sizes and varieties of smokestacks are available at craft shops.)

Two 12-ounce soft drink cans

Fifty-four wooden wheels (You can purchase wheels or cut them yourself. You'll need fifty wheels, each approximately ½ inch thick and 1½ inches in diameter, and four wheels of the same thickness, each 2 inches in diameter.)

Wooden axle pegs. (These can be purchased ready-made or you can make ordinary axles with plug ends. If you buy pegs, you'll need fifty four, each approximately 1¼ inches long, with a ¼-inch-diameter shank and ⅜-inch-diameter cap.)

Nine 6-inch lengths of pipe (steel or PVC plastic), approximately ⅝ inch in diameter (We used the pipe lengths to create something to load and unload from the flatbed car.)

6 feet of cotton string, about ¹⁄₁₆ inch in diameter

18-gauge wire brads: ½ inch and ¾ inch lengths

Two sheet metal screws, each ½ inch long

One internal-tooth washer with a ⅛-inch-diameter center hole

Several heavy-duty rubber bands

Carpenter's wood glue

Non-toxic paints in your choice of colors (We used red, green, yellow, orange, black, and white.)

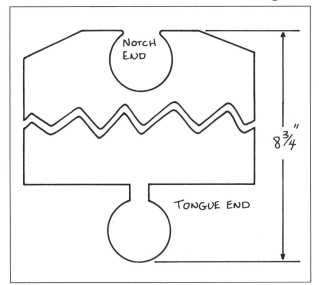

Figure A

CUTTING THE PIECES

Before you begin cutting, we suggest that you set aside a box or bin for each of the seven cars to hold the pieces in some kind of order until you're ready to assemble them.

Beds and Undercarriages

1. Although the engine and each of the six cars is different, all the cars are built on identical beds and undercarriages. For the Car Beds, cut six 3¼ x 9-inch pieces from 1 x 6. Full-size patterns for the tongue and notch ends of the Beds are provided in **Figure A**. Trace the patterns. Cut the tongue at one end (this will be the front end), and the notch at the opposite (rear) end of one Bed piece. Use this Bed as a pattern to cut four of the remaining Car Beds. (The last Bed will be modified for the Hopper Car, and the ends will be cut later.)

2. Each undercarriage consists of an H-shaped Frame and two Axle Supports. A full-size pattern for the Axle Support is provided in **Figure B**. Trace the pattern and cut twenty-four Axle Supports from 1 x 6. Drill a ¼-inch-diameter hole through each Support where indicated on the pattern. A cutting diagram for the undercarriage Frame is also provided in **Figure B**. Cut twelve Frames from ¼-inch plywood.

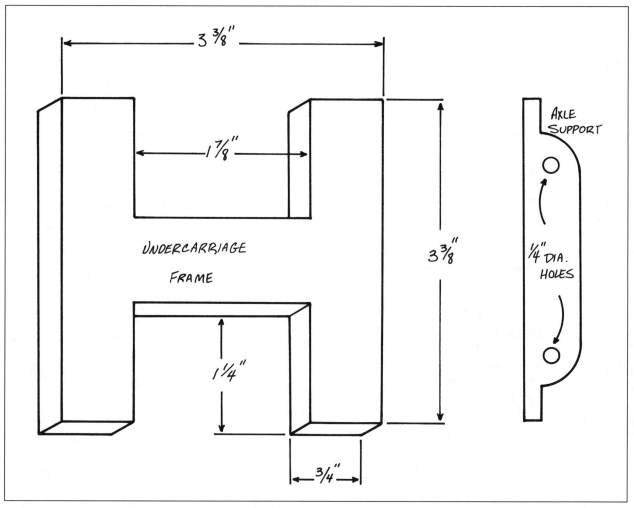

Figure B: UNDERCARRIAGE FRAME — 3⅜″ wide, 1⅞″ notch, 3⅜″ tall, 1¼″ and ¾″ dimensions. AXLE SUPPORT with ¼″ DIA. HOLES.

Engine

1. For the Engine Bed, cut a 3¼ x 9¾-inch piece from 1 x 6. Cut the rear notch in the same manner as you did the other Bed pieces. A full-size pattern for the Cowcatcher is provided in **Figure C**. Trace the pattern and cut one Cowcatcher from 1 x 6. Use the Cowcatcher as a pattern to cut the front end of the Engine Bed. The two short front edges of the Cowcatcher and Engine Bed are beveled at a 50-degree angle, as shown in **Figure D**. Cut the bevels on the Cowcatcher and the front end of the Engine Bed as shown.

2. For the engine cab, cut one 4¼ x 5-inch Roof from 1 x 6. A full-size pattern for the Cab Side Wall is provided in **Figure C**. Trace the pattern and cut two Cab Side Walls from ¼-inch plywood. Drill a ⅞-inch-diameter window hole through each Cab Side Wall where indicated. Cut one 3¼ x 4¼-inch Cab Front Wall from ¼-inch plywood. Cut a 2⅜-inch-diameter hole through the Front Wall, 2⅝ inches from one end and centered between the long edges.

3. The engine has different front and rear axle supports. For the Front Axle Support, cut a ⅞ x 3⅜-inch piece from 1 x 6. Drill a ¼-inch-diameter socket ¾ inch deep into each end, centered between the long edges

Figure C

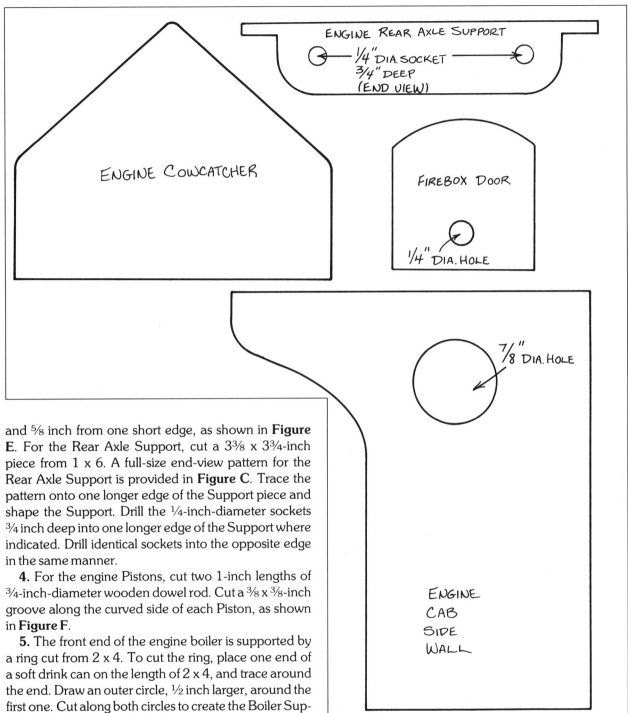

ENGINE REAR AXLE SUPPORT
1/4" DIA. SOCKET
3/4" DEEP
(END VIEW)

ENGINE COWCATCHER

FIREBOX DOOR

1/4" DIA. HOLE

7/8" DIA. HOLE

ENGINE
CAB
SIDE
WALL

and ⅝ inch from one short edge, as shown in **Figure E**. For the Rear Axle Support, cut a 3⅜ x 3¾-inch piece from 1 x 6. A full-size end-view pattern for the Rear Axle Support is provided in **Figure C**. Trace the pattern onto one longer edge of the Support piece and shape the Support. Drill the ¼-inch-diameter sockets ¾ inch deep into one longer edge of the Support where indicated. Drill identical sockets into the opposite edge in the same manner.

4. For the engine Pistons, cut two 1-inch lengths of ¾-inch-diameter wooden dowel rod. Cut a ⅜ x ⅜-inch groove along the curved side of each Piston, as shown in **Figure F**.

5. The front end of the engine boiler is supported by a ring cut from 2 x 4. To cut the ring, place one end of a soft drink can on the length of 2 x 4, and trace around the end. Draw an outer circle, ½ inch larger, around the first one. Cut along both circles to create the Boiler Support Ring. Drill a ¾-inch-diameter hole through

Figure D

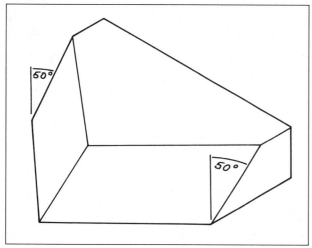

Figure E

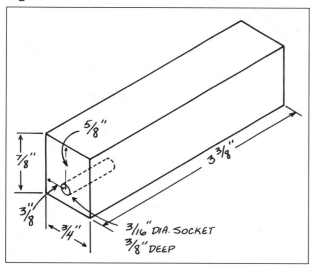

Figure F

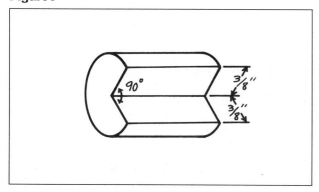

Figure G

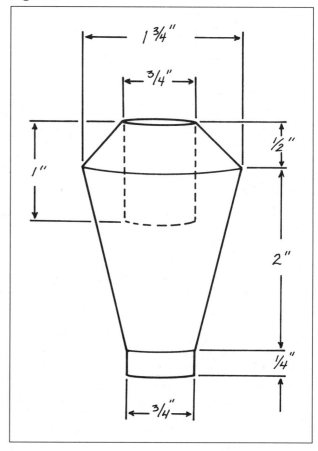

the Ring from the outer edge to the inner edge and centered between the sides, to accommodate the smokestack. A cutting diagram for the Smokestack is provided in **Figure G**.

6. For the Headlight, cut a 1¾-inch-diameter circle from 1 x 6. Bevel the curved edge all the way around at a 20-degree angle, as shown in **Figure H**.

7. For the Rear Boiler Wall, cut a 2⅜-inch-diameter circle from 1 x 6. A full-size pattern for the Firebox Door is provided in **Figure C**. Trace the pattern and cut one Firebox Door from ¼-inch plywood. Drill a ¼-inch-diameter hole through the Door where indicated. The Door swings in a notch cut into the Rear Boiler Wall. To cut the notch, place the Door on one side of the Wall, aligning the curved end of the Door with the edge of the Wall. Trace around the Door and cut the notch.

THE GREAT MECHANICAL WOODEN TOY BOOK

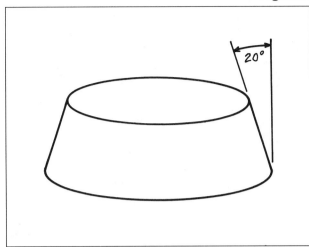

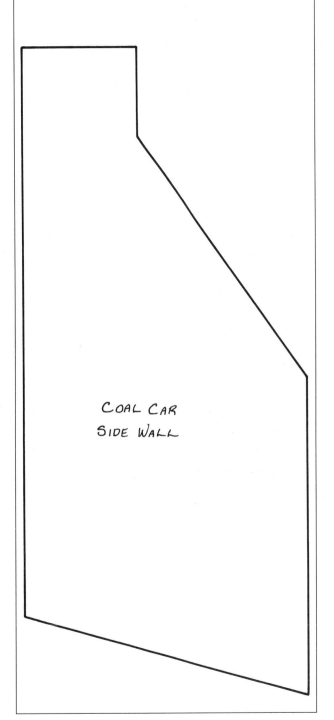

COAL CAR
SIDE WALL

Caboose, Coal, and Hopper Cars

1. Cut the pieces listed here from ½-inch pine. Label each piece to avoid confusion during assembly.

Description	Quantity	Dimensions
Coal Car Side Wall	2	3 x 7½ inches
Coal Car End Wall	1	2¼ x 3 inches
Hopper Car Side Wall	2	3¼ x 7¾ inches
Hopper Car End Wall	2	2 x 3¼ inches
Crane Cab Wall	2	3¼ x 3¼ inches
Caboose Doorway	2	2⅛ x 3¼ inches
Caboose Side Wall	2	3¼ x 4⅞ inches
Caboose Roof	1	3¼ x 7⅝ inches
Caboose Cupola Roof	1	3 x 3¼ inches

2. A full-size pattern for the Coal Car Side Wall is provided in **Figure I**. Trace the pattern and cut the contours on both Coal Car Side Walls. Bevel both ends of the Coal Car Back at a 15-degree angle, as shown in **Figure J**.

3. Cut notches in each Caboose Doorway and Side Wall, as shown in **Figure K**.

4. For the solid Caboose Cupola, cut a 2½ x 3¼-inch piece from 2 x 4. To form the windows, cut two ½ x ½-inch grooves across one side, from end to end, ½ inch from each edge, as shown in **Figure L**. Cut two additional grooves of the same size perpendicular to the first grooves, from edge to edge, ½ inch from each end.

Figure J

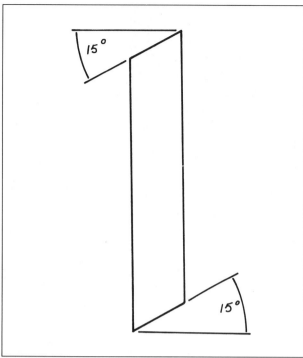

5. Cutting diagrams for the Hopper Car Side and End Walls are provided in **Figure M**. Shape each Side and End Wall as indicated. Bevel both ends of each End Wall at a 15-degree angle, as shown for the Coal Car Wall in **Figure J**. Bevel the shorter edge of each Side Wall at a 10-degree angle as shown in **Figure N**.

6. The Bed piece that was not contoured previously must be modified to accommodate the hopper car dumping mechanism, as shown in **Figure O**. We used a table saw to cut the grooves in the underside of the Bed. To begin, cut a $5/16$ x $2\frac{3}{8}$-inch groove from edge to edge, $2\frac{7}{8}$ inches from the rear end, as shown. Cut a $5/16$ x $1\frac{1}{2}$-inch groove from edge to edge in the middle of the first groove, as shown. (**Note:** if you're using a table saw to cut the grooves, set it at $5/8$ inch to cut the second groove.) Cut a $1\frac{1}{8}$ x 1-inch mortise through the center of the deeper groove, as shown. Cut a $1/8$ x $3/16$-inch notch in one edge, centered in the groove, as shown. Use another Car Bed as a pattern to cut the tongue and notch ends.

7. Cut a $2\frac{3}{8}$ x $3\frac{1}{4}$-inch hopper car Door Support from $1/4$-inch plywood. Cut a $1\frac{1}{4}$ x $1\frac{3}{8}$-inch mortise

Figure K

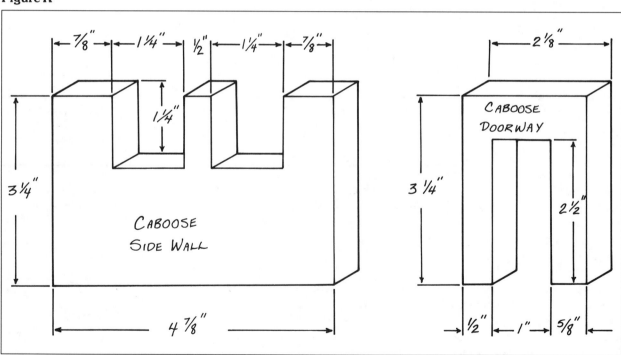

Figure L

through the center of the Support, as shown in **Figure P**. For the hopper car sliding Trap Door, cut a 1½ x 2½-inch piece from ¼-inch plywood. Drill a ⅛-inch-diameter pin hole through the Trap Door, ⅛ inch from one end and ⁹⁄₁₆ inch from one edge. Cut a ¾-inch length of ⅛-inch-diameter wooden dowel rod to serve as the Pin. Cut one ¾ x 1½-inch Spacer from ¼-inch plywood to fit between the Door Support and the underside of the Bed.

8. A full-size pattern for the Hopper Car Trap Door Lever is provided in **Figure Q**. For the Lever, rip a ⅜ x ¾ x 6-inch strip from 1 x 6. Trace the pattern and cut one Lever from the strip. Drill a ⅛-inch-diameter hole through the Lever where indicated. In addition, cut the Pin Slot where indicated.

Tank Car

1. The tank car has two Supports that are drilled to accommodate the tank, which is a painted soft drink can. For the Tank Supports, cut two 3¼-inch squares from 2 x 4. To drill the tank support sockets, center one end of a soft drink can on one side of one Support and trace around the rim of the can. We drilled the socket

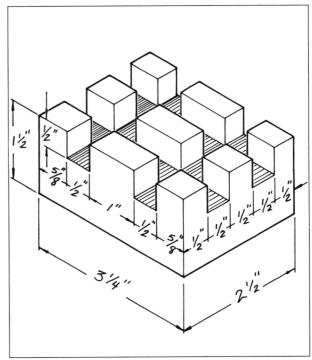

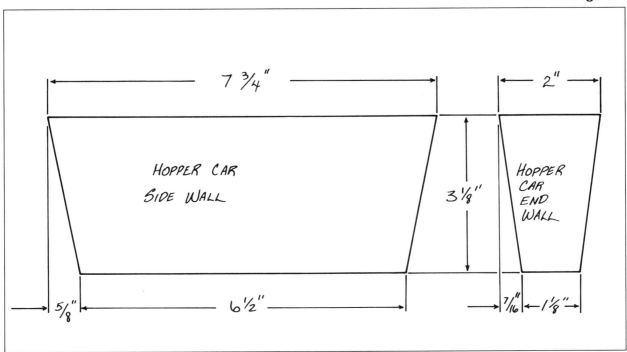

Figure M

Figure N

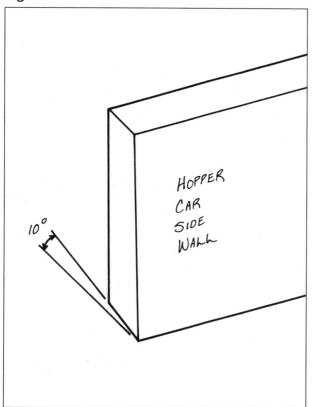

HOPPER
CAR
SIDE
WALL

10°

Figure P

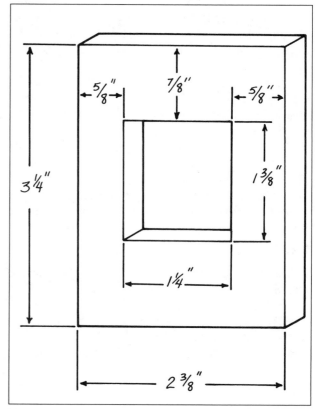

5/8"   7/8"   5/8"

3 1/4"

1 3/8"

1 1/4"

2 3/8"

Figure O

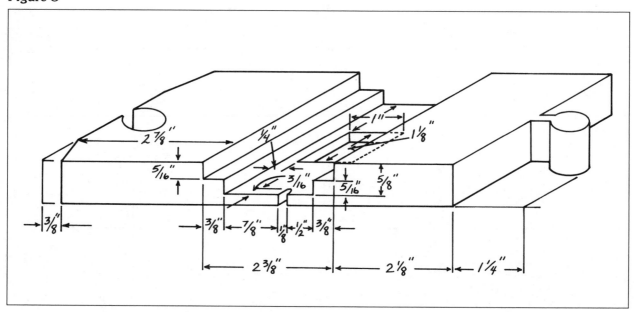

2 7/8"

1/4"

1"

1 1/8"

5/16"

3/16"

5/8"

5/16"

3/8"

3/8"   7/8"   1/8" 1/2" 3/8"

2 3/8"

2 1/8"

1 1/4"

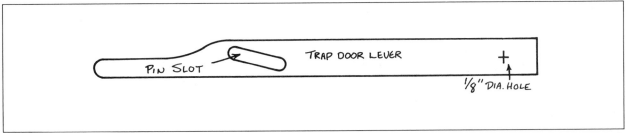

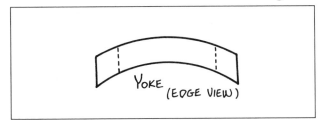

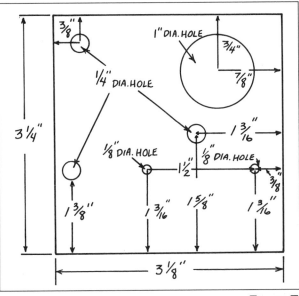

with a fly cutter, and chiseled out the center portion. Drill a ⅝-inch-deep socket into the Support, the same diameter as the can. Drill a socket of the same size into the remaining Support. The tank spigot pieces will be cut and drilled during assembly.

2. An intake hole in the tank is covered with a dowel rod Cap that fits into a wooden Neck, and a Yoke. For the Cap, cut a ¼-inch length of ¾-inch-diameter wooden dowel rod, and a matching length of 1-inch-diameter dowel. For the Neck, cut a ¾-inch length of 1-inch-diameter wooden dowel, and drill a ¾-inch-diameter hole through the center of the length. For the Yoke, cut a 1½-inch-diameter circle from 1 x 6, and drill a 1-inch-diameter hole through the center of the length. The Yoke is contoured to fit over the curved tank. A full-size pattern for the contour is provided in **Figure R**. Trace the pattern and cut the contour on one side of the Yoke.

Crane-Loader

1. You have already cut the Crane cab Walls. A drilling diagram for the Crane Cab Walls is provided in **Figure S**. To drill the holes in perfect alignment, temporarily nail the two Walls together, and drill the holes where indicated on the drawing.

2. A cutting diagram for the Crane Base is provided in **Figure T**. Cut one Crane Base from 1 x 6. For the

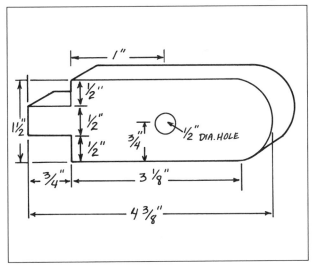

Figure U

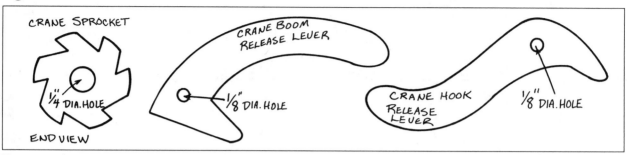

CRANE SPROCKET

CRANE BOOM
RELEASE LEVER

1/4" DIA. HOLE

1/8" DIA. HOLE

CRANE HOOK
RELEASE
LEVER

1/8" DIA. HOLE

END VIEW

Figure V

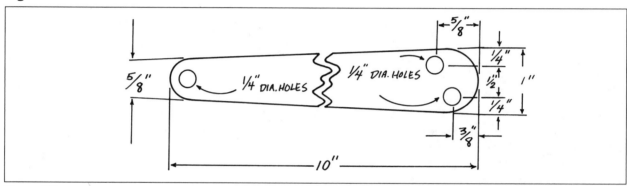

5/8"

1/4" DIA. HOLES

1/4" DIA. HOLES

5/8"

1/4"

1/2"

1/4"

1"

3/8"

10"

Figure W

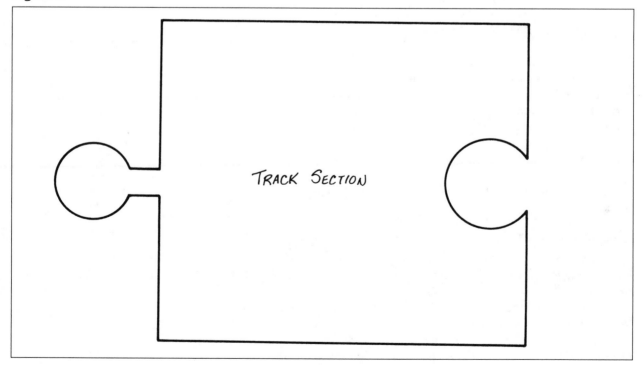

TRACK SECTION

Crane Sprockets, cut two 1½-inch lengths of 1-inch-diameter wooden dowel rod. Drill a ¼-inch-diameter hole through the center of each Sprocket from end to end. A full-size end-view pattern for the Sprocket grooves is provided in **Figure U**. Trace the pattern and cut the grooves from end to end along the curved edge of each Sprocket. In addition, drill a ⅛-inch-diameter hole through the middle of each Sprocket, perpendicular to the first hole.

3. For the crane car pieces you'll be cutting in this step, rip a 4-foot-long strip, ¼ inch thick and 1½ inches wide from 2 x 4. Full-size patterns for the Sprocket Release Levers are provided in **Figure U**. Trace the patterns and cut each Lever from the strip. Drill a ⅛-inch-diameter hole through each Lever where indicated on the pattern. A cutting diagram for the Crane Boom is provided in **Figure V**. Cut two Booms from the strip. Drill the ¼-inch-diameter holes through each Boom where indicated on the drawing. For the Center Boom, cut a ⅝ x 8½-inch piece from the remainder of the

Figure X

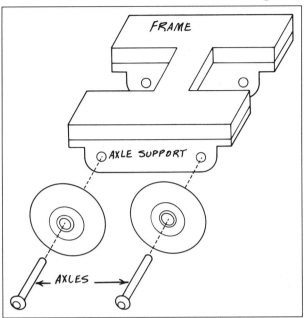

Figure Y

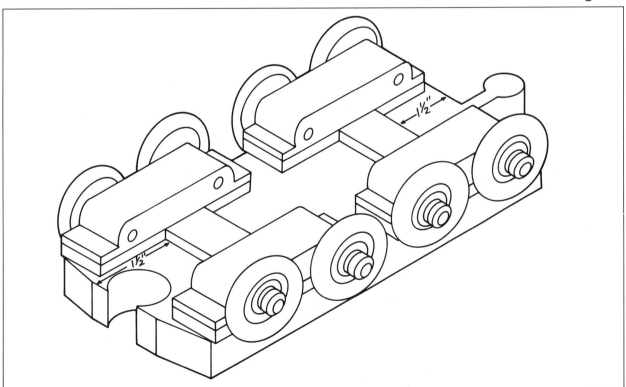

Figure Z

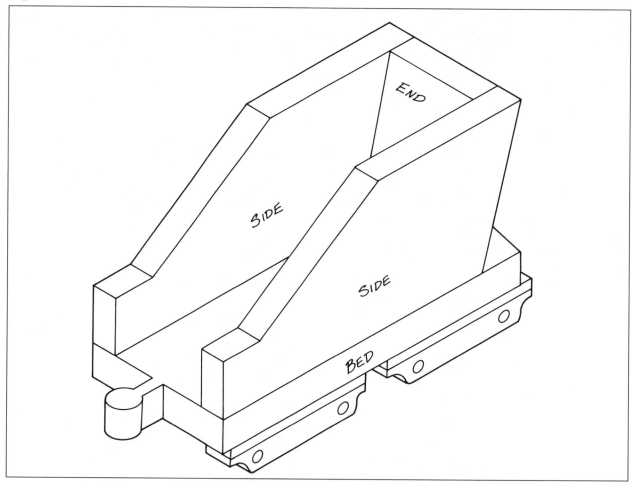

strip. Drill eight ¼-inch-diameter holes through the Center Boom, centered between the long edges. Drill the first hole ½ inch from one end, and space the remaining holes at 1-inch intervals.

Tracks

A full-size pattern for a Track Section is provided in **Figure W**. Trace the pattern and cut as many Track Sections as you like from ¼-inch waferwood. Cut short Track Sections for making curves, and longer ones for the straight-aways.

Assembly

If you're beginning to feel like a coolie working on the first transcontinental railroad, remember, you don't owe your soul to the company store yet! Assembling the train is almost as easy as slapping a model airplane kit together...and the result is much more rewarding. We'll start with the simplest cars so you can see what we mean – in no time!

Coal Car

1. The undercarriage assembly is shown in **Figure X**. To begin, attach one Axle Support to each leg of the Frame, using glue and ½-inch brads. File off any protruding brad points.

2. Assemble another identical undercarriage in the same manner.

3. To install one undercarriage assembly, place it against the underside of a Bed, so that the Frame crossbar is approximately 1½ inches from the front end of the Bed, as shown in **Figure Y**. Insert a ¾-inch brad through the Frame crossbar into the Bed, leaving the undercarriage loose enough to pivot on the brad.

4. Install the remaining undercarriage 1½ inches from the rear end of the Bed in the same manner.

5. The assembled coal car is shown in **Figure Z**. To begin, glue one Coal Car Side Wall to one side of the Bed flush with one long edge. The short front end of the Wall should be even with the tongue end of the Bed, as shown. Install the second Side Wall in the same manner, flush with the opposite edge of the Bed. Glue the Back Wall between the Side Walls, butting the edges as shown. Secure all joints with brads.

6. Install four 1½-inch-diameter Wheels on each undercarriage assembly, as shown in **Figure X**. Glue the Axle Pegs into the Axle Supports, but do not glue the Wheels to the Axle Pegs.

Flatbed Car

1. Assemble and install two undercarriages, as you did for the coal car.

2. Drill four ¼-inch-diameter sockets, each ½ inch deep, along each side of the Bed, as shown in **Figure AA**. The sockets should be placed ¼ inch from the edge, and spaced at 1½-inch intervals.

3. Cut eight 2-inch lengths of ¼-inch-diameter wooden dowel rod. Glue one length into each of the sockets that you drilled in step 2.

4. Install four 1½-inch-diameter Wheels on each undercarriage, as you did for the coal car.

Caboose

1. Assemble and install two undercarriages, as you did for the coal car.

2. The assembled caboose is shown in **Figure BB**. To begin, glue the two Doorway Walls between the two Side Walls as shown. To assemble the cupola, glue the

Figure AA

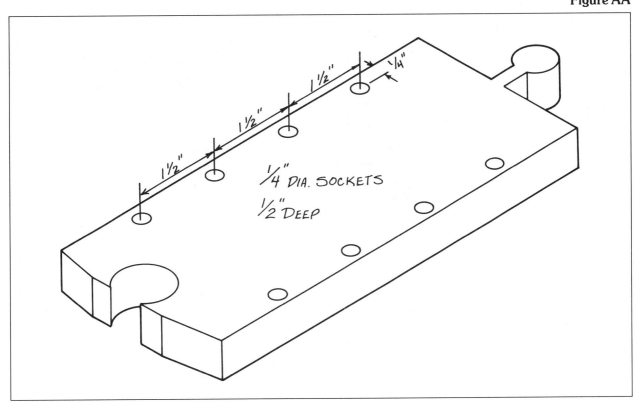

¼" DIA. SOCKETS
½" DEEP

Figure BB

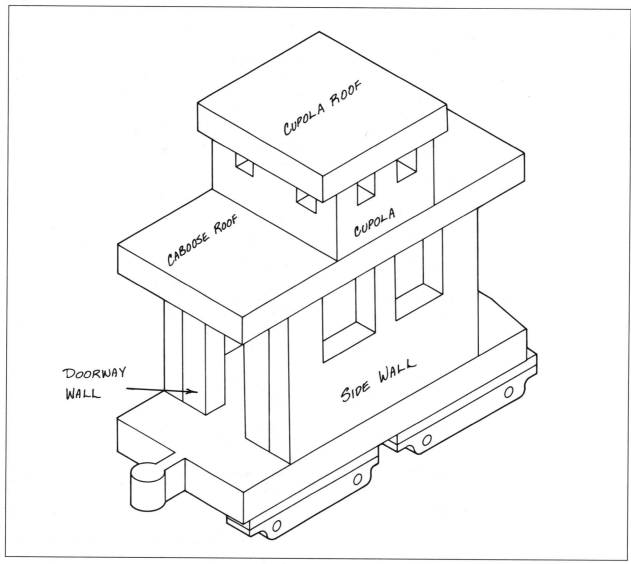

Cupola Roof to the grooved side of the Cupola. The Cupola Roof should extend equally beyond each long edge of the Cupola. Glue the assembled cupola to the Caboose Roof, centered between the ends, as shown. Attach the Caboose Roof to the upper edges of the Walls, leaving equal extensions at both ends, as shown. Install the entire assembly on the Bed, as shown.

3. Install four 1½-inch-diameter Wheels on each undercarriage, as you did for the coal car.

Engine

1. To install the Rear Axle Support, position it on the underside of the Engine Bed, so that the axle holes face outward, and the rear edge of the Support is ¼ inch from the notch in the Bed, (**Figure CC**). Insert a 1-inch brad through the center of the Support into the Bed, leaving the Support loose enough to pivot on the brad. To install the Front Axle Support, position it on the

Figure CC

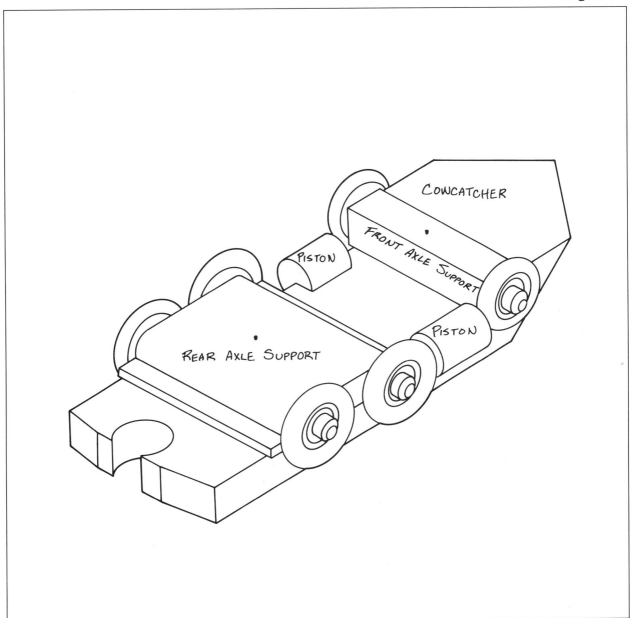

underside of the Bed just behind the Cowcatcher, so that the axle holes face outward and are farther from the Bed underside, as shown. Insert a 1-inch brad through the center of the Support into the Bed.

2. To install one Piston, place it midway between the front and rear axle supports, placing the groove against the edge and underside of the engine Bed, as shown in **Figure CC**. Glue the Piston in place. Install the remaining Piston on the opposite side of the Engine Bed in the same manner.

Figure DD

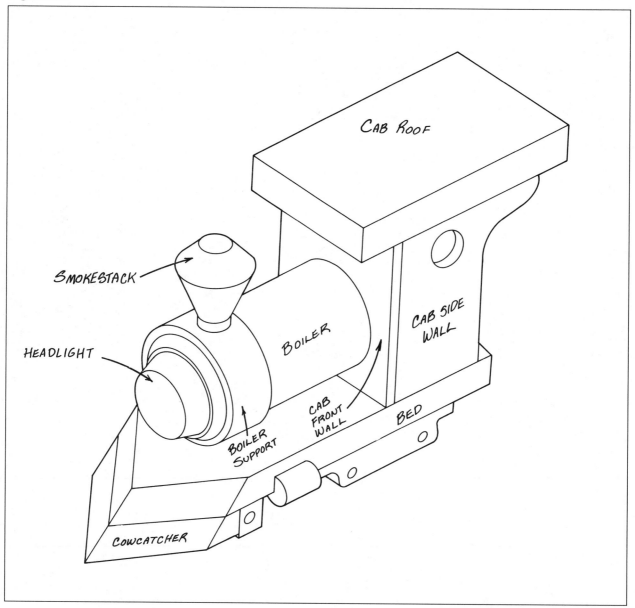

3. The assembled engine is shown in **Figure DD**. To begin, assemble the Cab Side and Front Walls, butting the edges as shown. The large hole (for boiler access) should be closer to the bottom of the assembly. Install the Cab Roof so that it extends equally over each Side Wall, and the front edge extends ½ inch over the Front Wall, as shown. Install the assembled engine cab on the Engine Bed, so that the Side Walls are ½ inch from the rear end of the Bed, as shown.

4. For the boiler, empty a soft drink can and cut off the end with the pop tab. Place the Headlight against the opposite end of the can and secure it by inserting

Figure EE

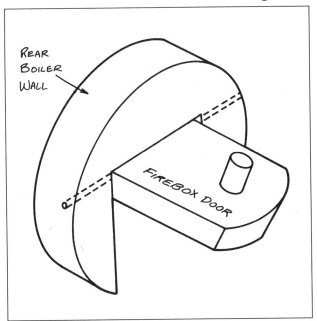

REAR BOILER WALL

FIREBOX DOOR

a screw from inside the can into the Headlight. To install the boiler on the engine, insert the open end into the hole in the Cab Front Wall. Slip the Boiler Support over the front end of the boiler can and slide it down until the front of the Support is even with the beveled end of the can, as shown. Rotate the Support so that the smokestack hole is at the top. Be sure the boiler is aligned properly, and glue the Support to the Bed.

5. To install the Smokestack, glue the lower end into the hole in the Boiler Support. To install the Cowcatcher, place it against the underside of the engine Bed so that the beveled edges are flush with the beveled edges of the Bed, as shown in **Figure DD**. Secure the Cowcatcher with glue and brads.

6. The Firebox Door hinges on brads inserted through the Rear Boiler Wall, as shown in **Figure EE**. To install the Firebox Door, place it into the notch in the Rear Boiler Wall, and insert a brad through the Wall edge into one edge of the Door, near the upper end, as shown. Install a brad on the opposite side of the Door

Figure FF

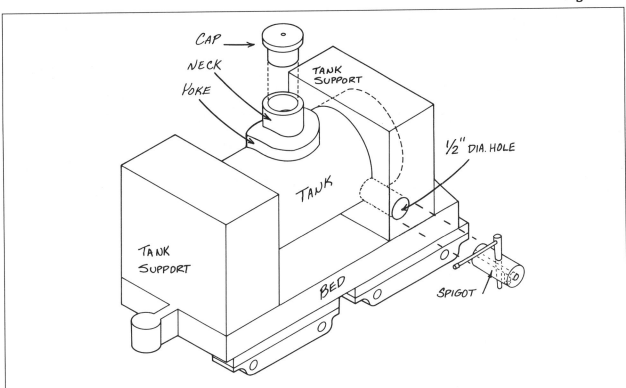

CAP

NECK

YOKE

TANK SUPPORT

TANK

½" DIA. HOLE

TANK SUPPORT

BED

SPIGOT

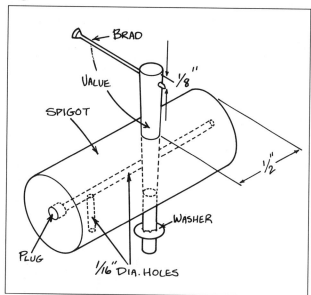

in the same manner. Glue the dowel Handle into the hole in the Firebox Door. To install this assembly in the Engine, insert it into the open end of the boiler so that the Firebox Door is on the bottom, and glue in place.

7. Install the Axle Pegs and Wheels in the same manner that you did for the coal car. Use the four 2-inch-diameter Wheels on the Rear Axle Support; use the smaller wheels on the Front Axle Support.

Tank Car

1. Assemble and install two undercarriages, as you did for the coal car.

2. The tank is a soft drink can mounted between two Supports, and this assembly is installed on a Bed. The tank is a real working model that you can fill through a hole in the top and empty through a spigot. Before you start, you'll need to empty a soft drink can – but don't open it in the usual way. Punch a small hole through the side of the can, 2½ inches from one end, and drain it. After you've enjoyed the drink, enlarge the hole to ¾ inch in diameter.

3. The intake hole is covered with a dowel rod cap that fits into the Neck and Yoke, which are glued to the tank, as shown in **Figure FF**. To begin, center the Yoke over the intake hole and glue in place. Insert one end

of the Neck into the Yoke hole, and push the Neck down until it is seated against the tank. Glue the Neck in place. To assemble the Cap, center the smaller diameter Cap piece on the larger-diameter piece and glue in place. Drill a ¹⁄₁₆-inch-diameter hole through the length of the assembled Cap.

4. The assembled tank car is shown in **Figure FF**. To begin, attach one Tank Support to the Bed, flush with the tongue end, so that the tank socket faces the notch end, as shown. Slip one end of the tank into the Support socket and glue in place. Be sure the intake hole is at the top, as shown. Slip the remaining Tank Support over the opposite end of the tank, and secure it to the tank and Bed.

5. For the Spigot, cut a 1¼-inch length of ½-inch-diameter wooden dowel rod. Drill a tapered valve hole through the Spigot ½ inch from one end, as shown in **Figure GG**. The valve hole tapers from ³⁄₁₆-inch-diameter on one side of the Spigot to ⅛-inch-diameter on the opposite side, as shown. (We ground down a ³⁄₁₆-inch-diameter bit and used it to drill the hole). Cut a 1⅛-inch length of ³⁄₁₆-inch-diameter dowel rod to serve as the Valve. Taper the Valve to match the tapered hole you drilled through the Spigot; the Valve extends through the hole ⅛ inch at the smaller end.

6. Insert one end of the Valve down into the valve hole, push the Valve through the hole and slip the internal-tooth washer over the end to secure it, as shown in **Figure GG**. For a Valve Handle, insert a 1-inch brad through the Valve ⅛ inch from the upper end, as shown. Turn the Valve so that the Handle is aligned with the Spigot and drill a ¹⁄₁₆-inch-diameter hole through the Spigot from end to end, as shown. In addition, drill a ¹⁄₁₆-inch-diameter spout hole into the curved side of the Spigot up into the first hole, as shown. To install the End Plug, enlarge the end hole in the Spigot to ⅛ inch in diameter, insert the Plug, and glue in place.

7. To install the Spigot, drill a ½-inch-diameter hole into the Tank, through the outer edge of one Tank Support, as shown in **Figure FF**. Drill the hole ¼-inch from the front of the Support and ¾ inch from the bottom, as shown. Glue the un-plugged end of the Spigot into the hole, so that the Valve Handle is on top, and the Spout hole is on the bottom, as shown.

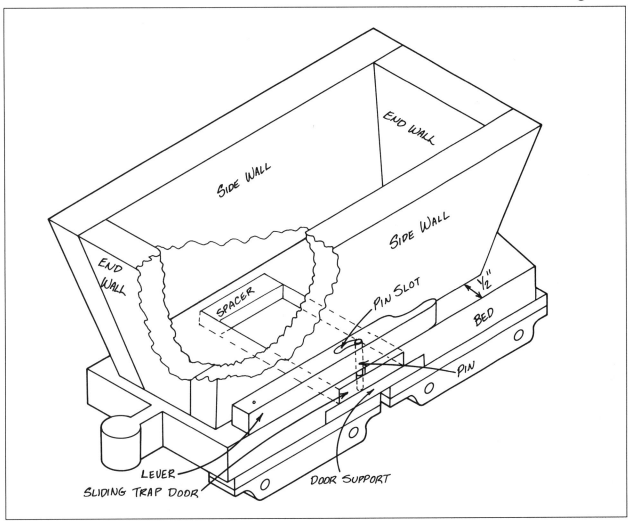

8. Install four 1½-inch-diameter Wheels on each undercarriage, as you did for the coal car.

Hopper Car

1. The assembled trap door mechanism is shown in **Figure HH**. To begin, glue the Spacer into the groove so that one edge is flush with the outer edge of the Bed that does not contain the lever notch. Glue the Door Support into the wider groove, and secure it with glue and brads. Insert one end of the Pin into the hole in the Trap Door and glue in place. Slide the Trap Door into

the slot on the edge of the Bed, as shown. To attach the Trap Door Lever, slip the pin slot over the upper end of the Trap Door Pin and position the Lever so that the longest edge is flush with the edge of the Bed, as shown. Insert a screw through the hole in the end of the Lever to secure it. To operate the trap door, simply pull the Lever out away from the Bed.

2. Assemble and install two undercarriages on the Hopper Car Bed, as you did for the coal car.

3. The assembled Hopper Car Side and End Walls are shown in **Figure HH**. To begin, attach one Side

Figure II

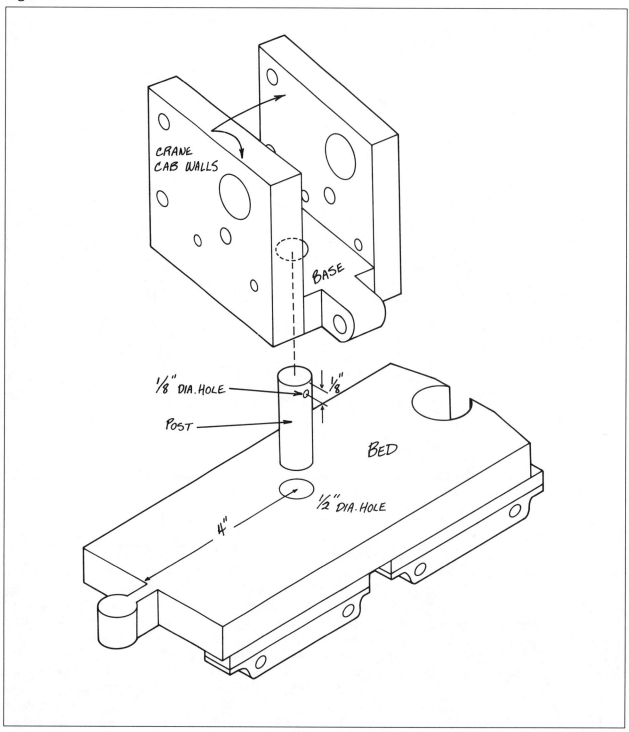

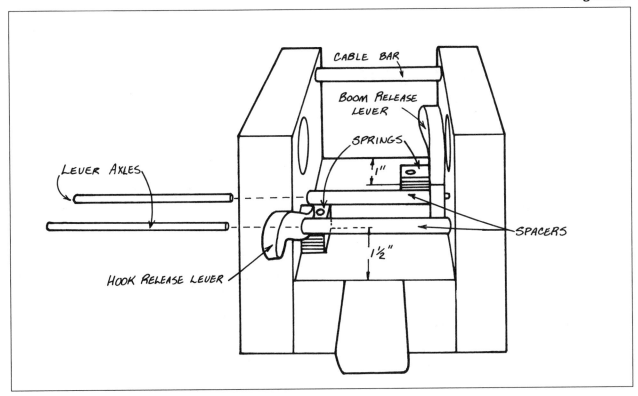

Wall, beveled edge down, to the Bed ½ inch from one edge, as shown. Attach the remaining Side Wall in the same position near the opposite edge of the Bed as shown. Attach the End Walls between the Side Walls, butting the edges as shown. The edges of the End Walls should be covered by the Side Walls.

4. Install four 1½-inch-diameter Wheels on each undercarriage, as you did for the coal car.

Crane Car

1. Assemble and install two undercarriages, as you did for the coal car.

2. Attach one Crane Cab Wall to each long edge of the Crane Base, so that the front of each Wall is flush with the notched front end of the Base, as shown in **Figure II**. Be sure the sockets in the Wall are facing toward the center, as shown.

3. To install the crane Base-and-Cab assembly on the remaining Bed, drill a ½-inch-diameter hole through the Bed, centered between the edges and 4 inches from the tongue end, as shown in **Figure II**. For the Pivot Post, cut a 1¾-inch length of ½-inch-diameter wooden dowel rod, and drill a ⅛-inch-diameter pin hole through it ⅛ inch from one end. Insert the undrilled end of the Pivot Post into the hole in the Bed and push it through the hole until the lower end is flush with the underside of the Bed. Glue the Pivot Post in place. Slip the Base over the extending upper end of the Pivot Post, and insert a short length of ⅛-inch-diameter dowel rod through the hole in the Pivot Post to keep the Base from coming off the Post.

4. To provide the spring action for the Boom Release and Hook Release Levers, cut the rubber bands into ½-inch pieces. Stack six or seven rubber band pieces to create a spring. Nail the spring to the Base with one edge along the drilled Cab Wall, as shown in **Figure JJ**. Create another spring in the same manner, and nail it to the Base so that one end is against the opposite Cab Wall, as shown.

Figure KK

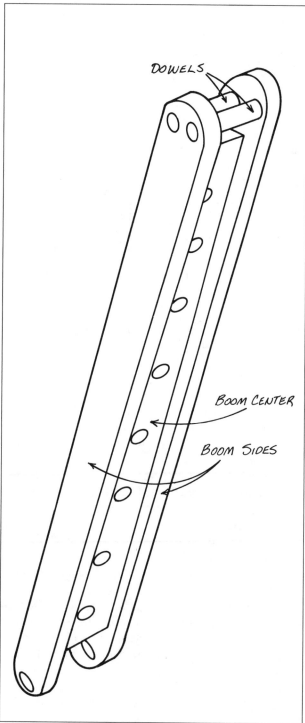

DOWELS

BOOM CENTER

BOOM SIDES

5. The Sprockets and Release Levers are installed on various dowel rod lengths that run between the two Cab Walls. Cut the following pieces from dowel rod:

Description	Quantity	Length	Dowel
Sprocket Axle	2	3 inches	¼-inch
Cable Bar	1	1½ inches	¼-inch
Spacer	2	1¼ inches	¼-inch
Lever Axle	2	2¼ inches	⅛-inch
Sprocket Handle	2	¼ inch	1-inch

6. Drill a ⅛-inch-diameter hole through the length of each Spacer from end to end. Drill a ¼-inch-diameter hole through the center of each Sprocket Handle.

7. To install the Hook Release Lever, insert one end of a Lever Axle through the upper Axle hole, as shown in **Figure JJ**. Push the Axle through the hole in the Hook Release Lever, through the hole in the Spacer, and into the socket in the opposite Wall, as shown. Install the Boom Release Lever on the inside of the opposite Wall in the same manner.

8. The two Sprockets are installed in the same manner. To install one Sprocket, insert one end of a Sprocket Axle into one of the lower ¼-inch-diameter holes in one Wall, as shown in **Figure LL**. Push the Axle through the hole in a Sprocket and into the hole in the opposite Wall, as shown. Slip a Sprocket Handle over one end of the Axle and glue in place. Install the remaining Sprocket in the same manner. Install the Cable Bar between the Cab Walls as shown.

9. To assemble the Boom, attach one Boom Side to each long edge of the Boom Center, aligning the holes in the upper and lower ends, as shown in **Figure KK**. Glue a 1¼-inch length of ¼-inch-diameter wooden dowel rod into each of the holes in the wider end.

10. To install the assembled Boom, position the narrower lower end over the extension on the Crane Base and align the holes, as shown in **Figure LL**. Cut a 1¼-inch length of ¼-inch-diameter dowel rod and insert one end into the hole. Glue the dowel rod to the Boom Sides, but not to the extension of the Base.

11. Cut the string into two 3-foot lengths. Tie one end of a piece of string through the hole in one Sprocket, and wind the Sprocket until most of the string is wound around it. Install the other piece of string on the opposite Sprocket in the same manner. Tie the free end

THE GREAT MECHANICAL WOODEN TOY BOOK

Figure LL

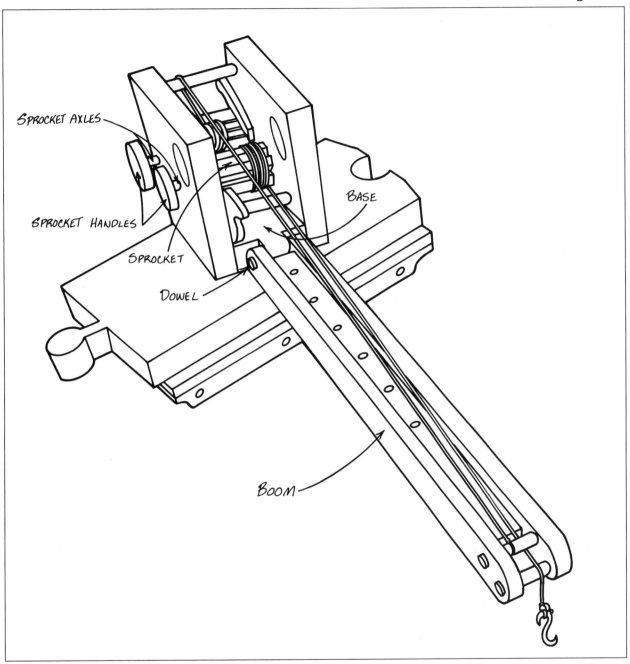

SPROCKET AXLES

SPROCKET HANDLES

SPROCKET

DOWEL

BASE

BOOM

of the Boom string to the lower Boom dowel rod, as shown in **Figure LL**. Thread the free end of the Hook string through the Boom dowel rods as shown and tie the hook to it.

12. Install four 1½-inch-diameter Wheels on each undercarriage, as you did for the coal car.

13. Paint the train carefully so that the moving parts will still move when the paint dries.

Whirling Ferris Wheel

Get your ticket right here...for a seat in the sky. From up on cloud nine, watch your child or grandchild gleefully escort the little dowel people to their seats, give them a ride (by turning the crank) and unload them one by one. Overall dimensions: 16 x 23 x 32 inches.

Materials

1-foot square of ⅛-inch plywood, finished on both sides

3-foot square of ¼-inch plywood, finished on both sides

4-foot square of ½-inch plywood, finished on both sides

8 linear feet of pine 1 x 6

3 linear inches of pine 2 x 4

Nine 3-foot lengths of ¼-inch-diameter wooden dowel rod

4-inch length of ½-inch-diameter wooden dowel rod

4½-inch length of ¾-inch-diameter wooden dowel rod

One 2-inch wooden axle peg, ¼-inch in diameter (Axle pegs are available at most hobby shops. If you prefer, you can create one by glueing a ⅛-inch length of ⅜-inch-diameter dowel rod to one end of a 1⅝-inch length of ¼-inch-diameter dowel.)

Twenty-one dowel people, each ¾ inch in diameter

Two heavy-duty rubber bands, each 2½ inches long

Carpenter's wood glue; 18 gauge wire brads, each ¾ inch long; two flathead sheet metal screws, each ½ inch long with flat washers to fit

Non-toxic paints in your choice of colors (We used red, yellow, orange, blue, green, brown, and black.)

Three ¾-inch-diameter plastic washers, each with a ¼-inch-diameter center hole (You can cut these from an old plastic bottle.)

One strand of a 10-inch length of 12 gauge copper wire or heavy thread

Beeswax

Cutting the Pieces

Note: Some of the pieces share the same code letters (for example, B Support and B Platform), so carefully label each piece with both the code letter and name.

1. The frame pieces are cut from 1 x 6, then grooved to look like steel I-beams, as shown in **Figure A**. For the frame pieces, rip a 1 x ¾-inch strip approximately 8 feet long from 1 x 6. (Do not discard the remaining piece.) Cut a ¾-inch-wide groove, ¼ inch deep from end to end along each side of the strip, centered ⅛ inch from both edges (**Figure A**). To cut the grooves, we used a table saw to cut two narrow grooves along both

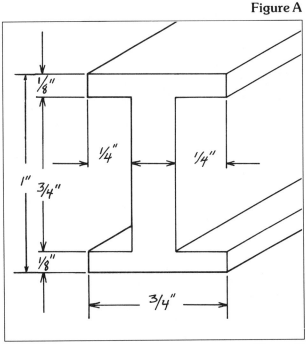

Figure A

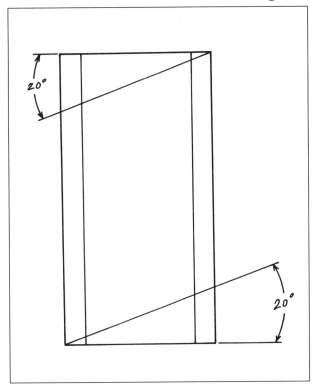

Figure B

Figure C

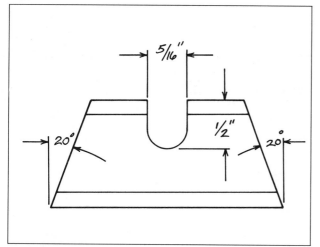

Figure D

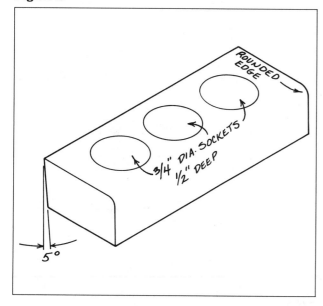

Figure E

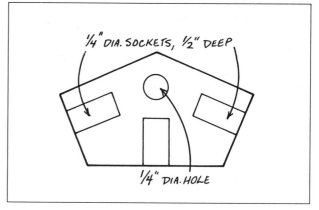

in **Figure B**. Miter both ends of each B Support at a 20-degree angle, as shown in **Figure C**. In addition, cut a ½ x ⁵⁄₁₆-inch notch into the short edge of each B Support, as shown.

3. For the Seats, rip a 1³⁄₈ x ³⁄₄-inch strip approximately 3 feet long, from the remainder of the 1 x 6. Cut eight Seats, each 3³⁄₄ inches long, from the strip. Round off one edge of each Seat (this will be the upper front edge). Bevel the back edge of each Seat at a 5-degree angle, as shown in **Figure D**. Drill a ³⁄₄-inch-diameter socket ½ inch deep into the center of one Seat (the socket will hold a dowel person). Drill another Seat in the same manner. Drill two sockets into each of four additional Seats, spacing the holes evenly between the Seat ends. Drill three sockets into each of the two remaining Seats, spacing them evenly.

4. A full-size pattern for the Seat Support is provided in **Figure E**. Trace the pattern and cut one Seat Support from 1 x 4. Use this Support as a guide to cut fifteen identical Seat Supports. Drill a ¼-inch-diameter hole through each Seat Support where indicated on the pattern. In addition, drill ¼-inch-diameter sockets ½ inch deep into both ends and the long edge of each Support, as shown.

5. For the Wheel Hubs, cut two 3½-inch lengths of 1 x 6 and nail them together temporarily. Cut two 3-inch-diameter Hubs simultaneously, and drill a ¼-inch-diameter hole through the exact center of each Hub. Remove the temporary holding nails, and drill eight evenly spaced ¼-inch-diameter sockets, ½ inch deep, into the curved edge of each Hub.

sides of the piece, then we moved the saw blade over by ⅛-inch increments and made repeated passes along both sides to widen the grooves. From the grooved strip, cut four Rails, each 16¼ inches long, four A Supports, each 12½ inches long, and two B Supports, each 2¼ inches long.

2. The A and B Supports must be mitered at both ends so that they will fit together properly. Miter one end of each A Support at a 20-degree angle, as shown

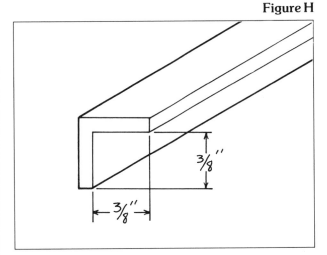

7. A cutting diagram for the Gear Support is provided in **Figure G**. Cut one Gear Support from 1 x 6, and drill three ¼-inch-diameter holes where indicated.

8. For a Belt Guard, cut a ½ x ½ x 3½-inch piece from 1 x 6. Cut a ⅜ x ⅜-inch groove along one edge, as shown in **Figure H**.

6. A full-size pattern for the Gear is provided in **Figure F**. Trace the pattern and cut two Gears from 1 x 6. Drill a ¼-inch-diameter hole through the exact center of each Gear.

9. The pulleys consist of Rims and Hubs. For the Rims, cut five 3½-inch squares from ⅛-inch plywood. Temporarily nail the squares together and cut five 3-inch-diameter Rims. Cut four 2-inch-diameter Pulley

Figure G

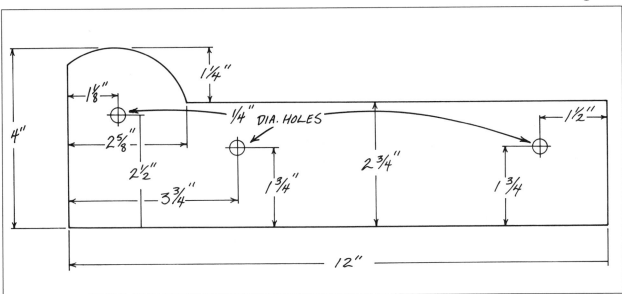

Figure I

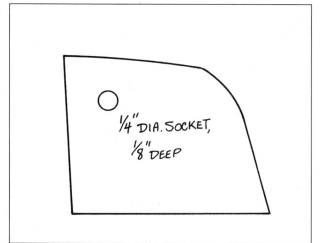

1/4" DIA. SOCKET,
1/8" DEEP

Figure J

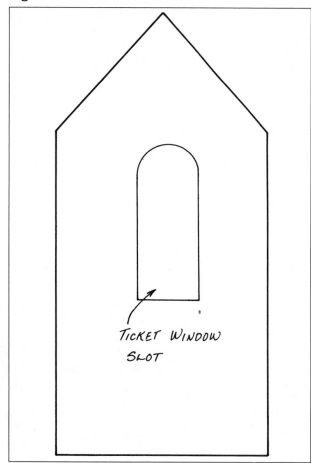

TICKET WINDOW
SLOT

Figure K

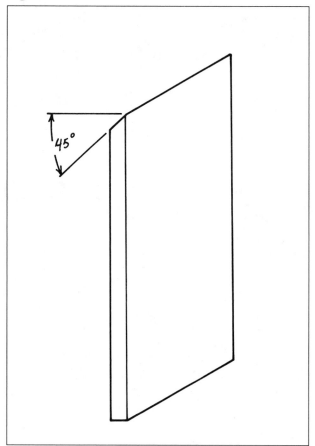

45°

Hubs from 1/4-inch plywood in the same manner. Drill a 1/4-inch-diameter hole through the exact center of each Pulley Rim and Hub. Cut one 3-inch-diameter Crank Rim from 1/4-inch plywood, and drill a 1/4-inch-diameter hole through it 1/4 inch from the edge.

10. For the Seat Back/Floor, cut sixteen 2 1/4 x 3 3/4-inch pieces from 1/4-inch plywood. Round off one long edge of each Seat Back/Floor.

11. A full-size pattern for the Seat Wall is provided in **Figure I**. Trace the pattern and cut sixteen Seat Walls from 1/4-inch plywood. Drill a 1/4-inch-diameter socket 1/8 inch deep, where indicated on the pattern, into eight of the Walls. Drill an identical socket into the opposite side of each of the remaining Walls.

12. For the ticket booth, cut the pieces listed here from 1/4-inch plywood.

THE GREAT MECHANICAL WOODEN TOY BOOK

Figure L

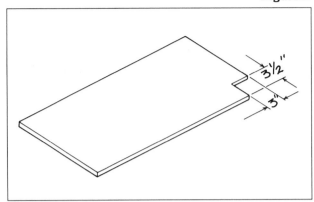

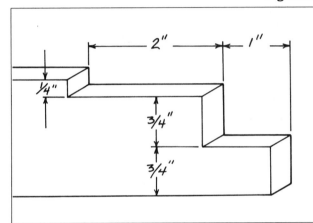

Figure M

Description	Quantity	Dimensions
Booth Platform	1	3 x 4 inches
Side Wall	2	2 x 3⅝ inches
End Wall	2	2¼ x 4⅝ inches
A Roof	1	1⅞ x 2⅞ inches
B Roof	1	2⅛ x 2⅞ inches
Shelf	1	⅝ x 1 inch

13. The Side and End Walls that you cut in step 12 must be modified. A full-size pattern for the End Wall is provided in **Figure J**. Trace the pattern and cut the peak on both End Walls; cut the ticket window slot through one End Wall only. Bevel one end of each Side Wall at a 45-degree angle, as shown in **Figure K**.

14. Cut one 1¾ x 2-inch Ticket Booth Floor from 1 x 6. Drill a ¾-inch-diameter socket ½ inch deep into one side of the Floor, centered between the edges and ¾ inch from one end.

15. Cut the pieces listed here from ½-inch plywood.

Description	Quantity	Dimensions
Ramp	6	4¾ x 10 inches
A Platform	1	16 x 32 inches
B Platform	2	1¾ x 32 inches
C Platform	1	1¾ x 15 inches
D Platform	1	1¾ x 12 inches
E Platform	1	1¾ x 2½ inches

Figure N

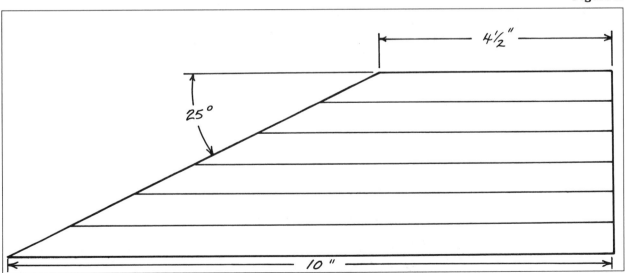

Figure O

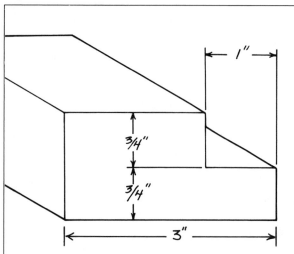

Figure P

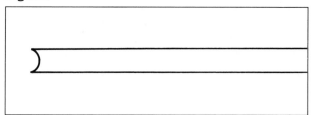

16. Cut a 3 x 3½-inch notch from one corner of the A Platform, as shown in **Figure L**.

17. One B Platform piece must be notched to accommodate the stairs. A cutting diagram for the stair notches is provided in **Figure M**. Cut the notches in one end of a B Platform piece where indicated.

18. To create the ramp, stack the six Ramp pieces and glue them together. After the glue is dry, miter one

Figure Q

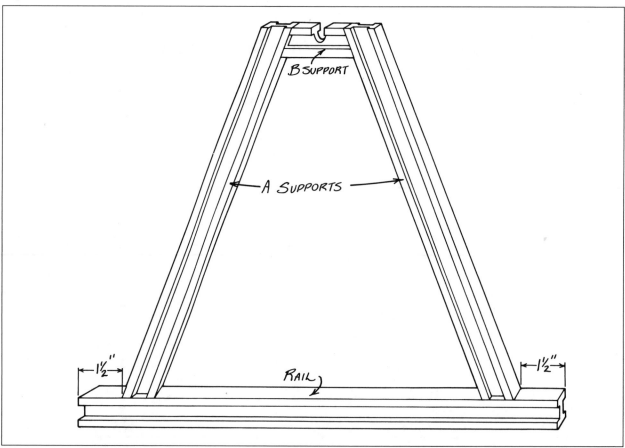

THE GREAT MECHANICAL WOODEN TOY BOOK

end of the ramp at a 25-degree angle, as shown in **Figure N** (we used a band saw to make the cut). Drill three ¾-inch-diameter sockets into the mitered end of the Ramp, perpendicular to the bottom, for waiting riders.

19. The 3-inch length of 2 x 4 will serve as the Steps. A cutting diagram is provided in **Figure O**. Cut the grooves across one end of the 2 x 4 to create the stairs, as shown. For the Top Step, cut a 1 x 3½ x ¾-inch piece from 1 x 6. Drill a ¼-inch-diameter socket into the center of the lowest stair of the 2 x 4 Steps, and another into the center of the Top Step, to accommodate Posts.

20. Cut and label the lengths of ¼-inch-diameter dowel listed here.

Code	Quantity	Length
A Rod	16	7½ inches
B Rod	16	5¾ inches
C Rod	8	5¼ inches
D Rod	16	1⅛ inches
Axle	1	9 inches
A Gear Shaft	2	1¾ inches
B Gear Shaft	1	1½ inches
Post	4	1½ inches

21. Both ends of each C Rod must be contoured. A full-size pattern for the contour is provided in **Figure P**. Trace the pattern and contour both ends of each C Rod. Round off one end of each D rod. Drill a ¹⁄₁₆-inch-diameter hole through each Post, ¼ inch from one end.

22. Cut two ⅝-inch-long End Spacers from ½-inch-diameter wooden dowel rod. Drill a ¼-inch-diameter hole through the center of each End Spacer from end to end. Drill the same size hole through the center of the length of ¾-inch-diameter dowel, which will serve as the Center Spacer.

23. For the Crank, cut a 1½-inch-long Sleeve from ½-inch-diameter wooden dowel rod. Drill a ¼-inch-diameter hole through the center of the Sleeve from end to end. The 2-inch peg will serve as the Crank Shaft.

Assembly

1. One side of the assembled support frame is shown in **Figure Q**. To begin, attach an A Support 1½ inches from each end of one Rail, turning each one so that it tilts toward the middle of the Rail, as shown. Attach a

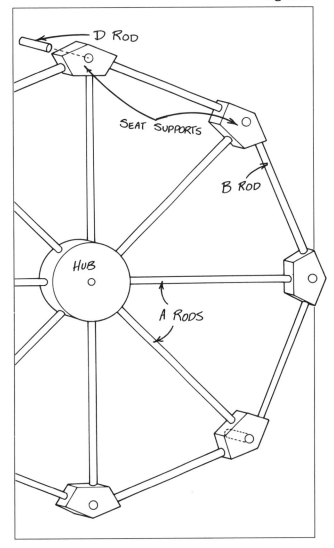

B Support between the upper ends of the A Supports so that the notch faces up, as shown. Build an identical support frame in the same manner.

2. One side of the assembled wheel is shown in **Figure R**. To begin, insert an A Rod into each socket in the Wheel Hub. Insert the opposite end of each A Rod into the socket in the long edge of a Seat Support, as shown. Install a B Rod between each pair of Seat Supports, inserting each end completely into a socket, and glue in place. Insert a D Rod into the hole in each Seat Support

Figure S

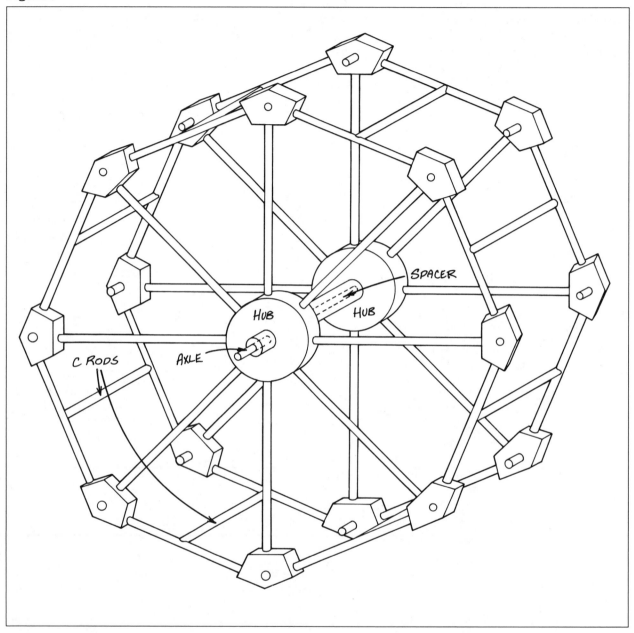

so that the flat end of the rod is flush with one side of the Support, and glue in place. All rods should extend from the same side of the assembled wheel, as shown. Build an identical wheel in the same manner, but do not glue the D Rods in place on the second wheel.

3. The assembled wheel is shown in **Figure S**. To begin, insert the Axle through the hole in the Center Spacer leaving equal extensions at each end. Slip an assembled wheel over each end of the Axle, as shown, and slide them together until the Hubs are butted

THE GREAT MECHANICAL WOODEN TOY BOOK

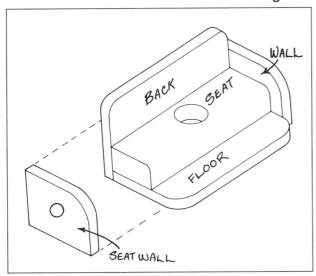

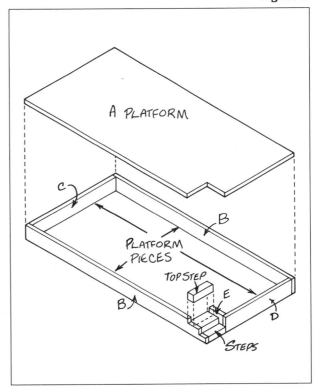

against the Spacer ends. Note that the D Rods should extend toward the center. The C Rods serve as spacers between the two wheels and are attached between facing B Rods, as shown. To install one C Rod, glue one contoured end to the middle of one B Rod and drive a brad through the B Rod into the end of the C Rod. Rotate the wheel until the Seat Supports on both wheels are aligned, and attach the opposite end of the C Rod to the middle of the facing B Rod, as shown. Install the remaining C Rods in the same manner. Slip an End Spacer over each end of the Axle.

4. One assembled seat is shown in **Figure T**. To begin, attach a Seat to a Floor so that the ends are flush and the beveled edge of the Seat is flush with the back edge of the Floor, as shown. Attach a Back to the Seat and Floor, butting the edges as shown. The Back covers the rear edge of the Floor. Attach a Seat Wall to each end of the assembly, with the socket facing outward, as shown. Assemble seven additional seats in the same manner.

5. The assembled platform is shown in **Figure U**. Assemble a frame using the B, C, D, and E Platform pieces, butting the edges as shown. The B pieces cover the ends of the C piece and one end of the D piece; there is a gap between the stair-cut B piece and the E piece. Attach the A piece to the upper edges of the assembled platform frame so that the stairway notch is aligned with the stair-cut B piece, as shown.

6. To attach the Steps, align the stairs with the stair notches in the assembled platform frame, and nail the Steps to the B and E pieces, as shown in **Figure U**. Nail the Top Step to the Steps so that the upper side is flush with the top of the platform, as shown.

Final Assembly

1. Install one assembled support frame on the platform, 6 inches from the platform edge, so that one end of the frame is flush with the platform end opposite the stairway, as shown in **Figure V**. Install the other support frame in the same manner, 6⅝ inches from the first one, as shown.

2. To install the assembled wheel, place it between the frames so that the Axle extensions rest in the notches in the B Supports, as shown in **Figure V**. The end of the Axle on the side of the wheel that faces the center of the platform should extend ¾ inch beyond the support frame, as shown.

Figure V

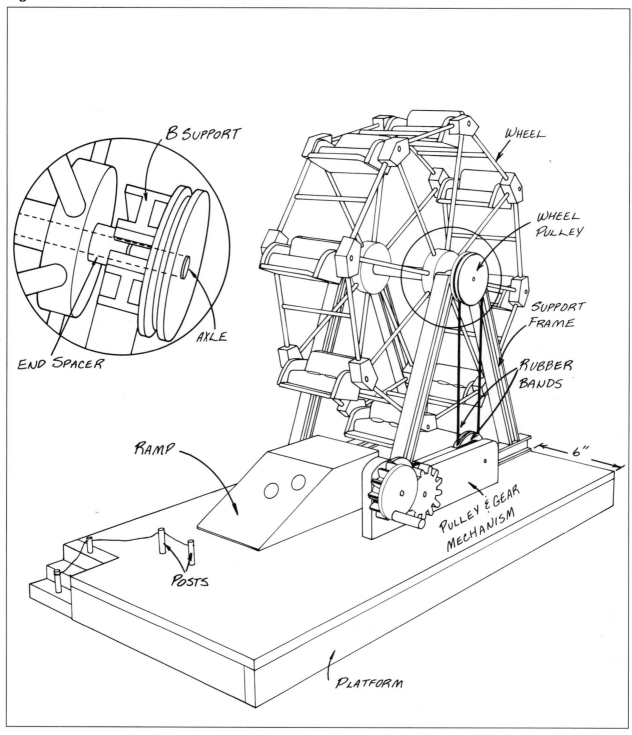

B SUPPORT

WHEEL

WHEEL PULLEY

SUPPORT FRAME

RUBBER BANDS

AXLE

END SPACER

RAMP

6"

PULLEY & GEAR MECHANISM

POSTS

PLATFORM

THE GREAT MECHANICAL WOODEN TOY BOOK

Figure W

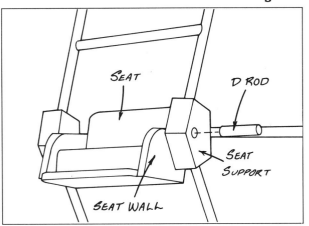

3. To install one seat, pull the unglued D Rod in one Seat Support out of its hole. Position the seat between two facing Seat Supports, slipping it onto the glued D Rod, as shown in **Figure W**. Re-insert the unglued D Rod you removed earlier, and push it through the Seat Support until it engages in the socket on the Seat Wall, as shown. Glue the D Rod to the Seat Support, but not into the Seat Wall. Install the remaining seats in the same manner. So that the wheel is balanced, install identical seats on opposite sides of the wheel, for example, a one-seater opposite another one-seater.

4. The assembled pulley and gear mechanism is shown in **Figure X**. To begin, insert an A Gear Shaft into the center hole in one Gear, so that one end is flush

Figure X

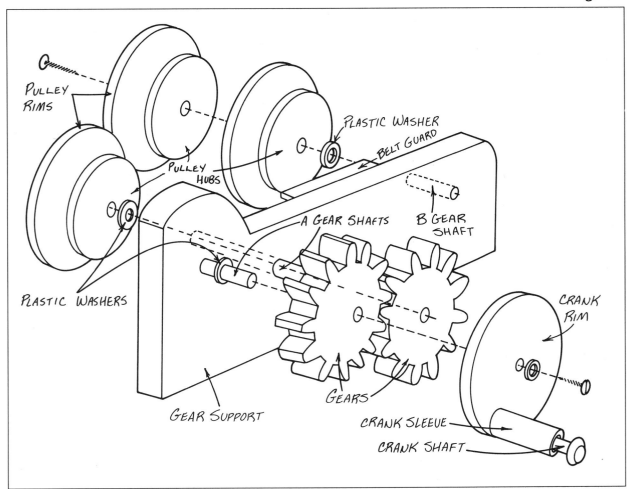

Figure Y

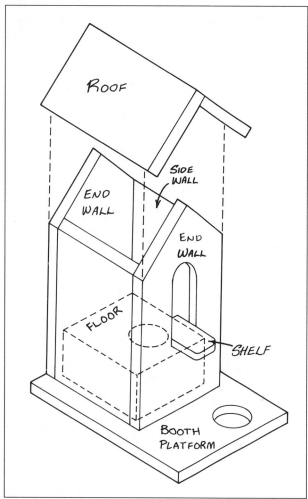

ROOF

SIDE WALL

END WALL

END WALL

FLOOR

SHELF

BOOTH PLATFORM

with one side of the Gear, and glue in place. To install the Gear, insert the Gear Shaft into the center hole in the Gear Support, so that the Gear is against one side of the Support (this will be the front of the Support). On the end of the Gear Shaft that extends from the back side of the Gear Support, install a plastic washer, a Pulley Hub, and a Pulley Rim, as shown. Glue the Pulley Hub and Rim to the Gear Shaft, but do not glue the Gear Shaft to the Gear Support. Glue the remaining A Gear Shaft into the upper hole in the Gear Support, so that one end is flush with the back side of the Support. Slip a plastic washer, one Gear, and the Crank Rim over the extending end of the Shaft and insert a screw

with a washer into the end of the Shaft, as shown. Glue the B Gear Shaft into the remaining hole in the Gear Support, so that one end is flush with the front side of the Support, as shown. To assemble the last pulley, slip a plastic washer, a Pulley Hub, a Pulley Rim, another Pulley Hub, and another Pulley Rim onto the B Gear Shaft, and insert a screw with a washer into the end of the Shaft, as shown. Glue a Pulley Rim, Hub, and Rim on the ferris wheel Axle, so that the Axle end is flush with the outer Rim. To install the Crank, slip the Sleeve over the Crank Shaft and glue the end of the Shaft into the hole near the edge of the Crank Rim. Install the Belt Guard on the back side of the Gear Support, midway between the pulleys, so that one edge is flush with the top of the Gear Support, as shown.

5. Install the assembled gear and pulley mechanism on the platform so that the end pulley is directly under the pulley on the ferris wheel, as shown in **Figure V**. The Gear Support should be 1 inch from the wheel support frame. Install one rubber-band belt between the pulleys on the Gear Support, as shown. Install the remaining rubber band between the pulley on the wheel and the pulley directly below it, as shown.

6. The assembled ticket booth is shown in **Figure Y**. Assemble the Side and End Walls around the Floor, butting the edges as shown. The End Walls cover the edges of the Side Walls, and all lower ends are flush. Install the Shelf in the ticket window, and install the assembled booth on the Booth Platform, so that the window faces the end with the hole, as shown. Assemble the two Roof pieces, butting the edges as shown. Place the roof on top of the ticket booth, but do not glue it, or the kids will go mad trying to place a little dowel person in the ticket booth.

7. To install the Ramp, position it between the support frame pieces so that the higher end is even with the supports, as shown in **Figure V**.

8. Install the Posts in the stairway sockets, as shown in **Figure V**. Thread the wire or thread through the holes to serve as a guide rope, and secure the ends.

9. Paint the ferris wheel with bright summertime colors, but be sure to keep paint off of moving parts so that they won't stick together. After painting, rub beeswax on the gear teeth, wheel axle, and Seat Support Rods so they'll turn more smoothly.

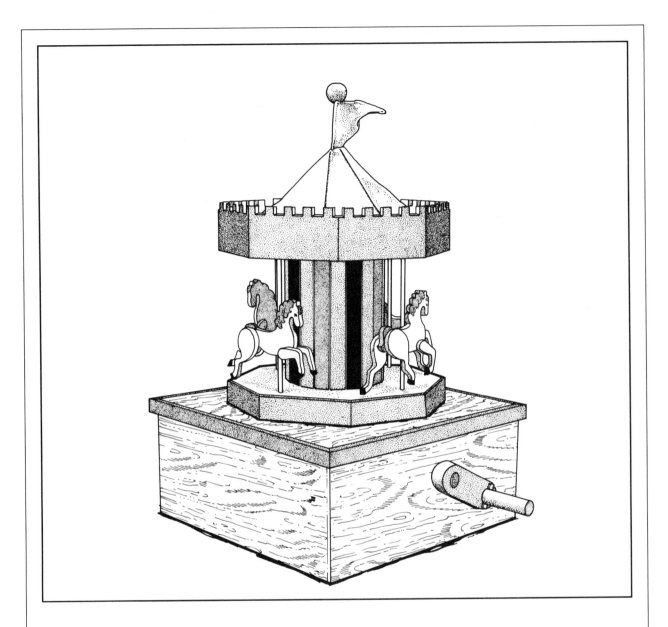

Spinning Carousel

Help wanted: carousel operator. Must be able to turn crank and be willing to play long hours for no pay. Unlimited opportunity for fun. Active imagination a plus. Children only need apply. Overall dimensions: 15 x 15 x 24 inches.

Materials

13 x 24-inch piece of ¼-inch interior plywood, finished on both sides

2 x 4-foot piece of ½-inch interior plywood, finished on both sides

8 linear feet of pine 1 x 6

1 linear foot of pine 2 x 4

9-inch length of 18-inch-diameter wooden dowel rod

6-foot length of ¼-inch-diameter wooden dowel rod

2-inch length of ½-inch-diameter wooden dowel rod

10-inch length of ¾-inch-diameter wooden dowel rod

5-inch length of 1½-inch-diameter wooden closet rod

One spherical wooden drawer pull, 1 inch in diameter

¼ yard of canvas (We used beige.)

3 x 5 -inch piece of felt (We used pink.)

10-inch length of floral wire

18 gauge wire brads: ½ inch and 1 inch lengths

No. 6 gauge flathead wood screws, each 1 inch long

Carpenter's wood glue; hot-melt glue and a glue gun, or white glue

Figure A

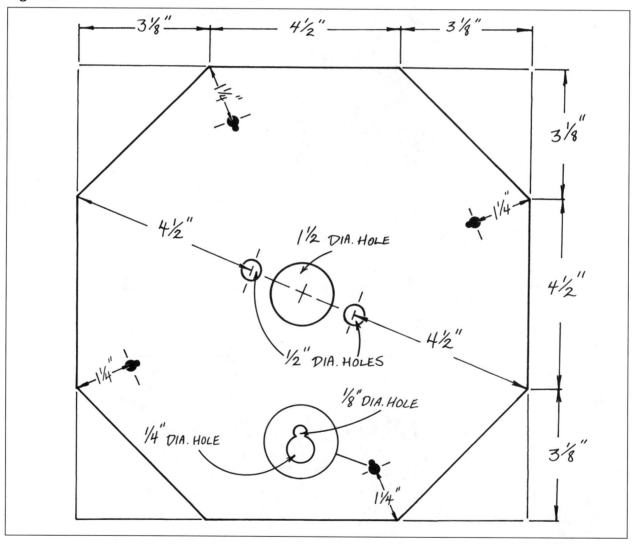

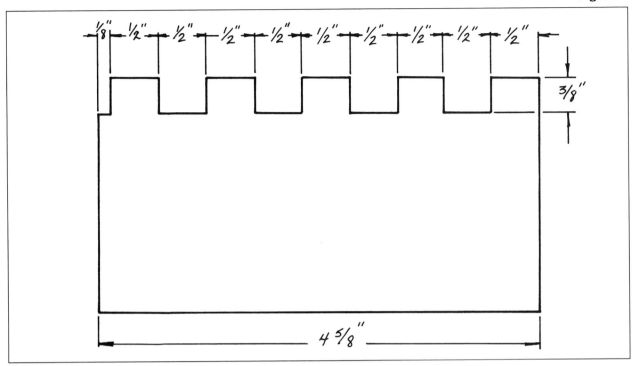

Cutting the Pieces

1. Cut the pieces listed here from ½-inch plywood. Label each piece as it's cut to avoid confusion while you're in the throes of assembly.

Description	Quantity	Dimensions
A Platform	2	6 x 14 inches
B Platform	2	6 x 13 inches
C Platform	1	14 x 14 inches
Ring	2	4¾-inch diameter
Floor/Ceiling	2	10¾ x 10¾ inches

2. Drill a ¾-inch-diameter hole through one **A** Platform piece, centered between the ends, and 2 inches from one edge.

3. Drill a 1½-inch-diameter hole through the center of the **C** Platform piece.

4. Each Floor/Ceiling must be cut into an octogon shape, and drilled to accommodate the horse poles. A cutting diagram for the Floor/Ceiling pieces is provided in **Figure A**. Cut each Floor/Ceiling as indicated. To

drill the ¼-inch-diameter holes, temporarily nail the two pieces together. Drill these holes where indicated. Remove the temporary holding nails, and drill the ⅛-inch-diameter holes in the Floor only. In addition, drill the ½-inch and 1½-inch-diameter holes through the Floor only, where indicated.

5. Cut a 3½-inch-diameter circle out of the center of the Ring.

6. For the Ceiling Trim, cut eight 2½ x 4⅝-inch pieces from ¼-inch plywood. A cutting diagram for the notches in the Trim is provided in **Figure B**. Cut the notches in each Ceiling Trim piece. Place the Ceiling Trim pieces end to end, as shown in **Figure C**. The outer side of each piece should be facing you. Bevel both ends of each Ceiling Trim piece at a 20-degree angle toward the inner side, as shown in **Figure D**.

7. For Ceiling Trim Supports, rip a ¾ x ¾-inch strip, approximately 3 feet long, from 1 x 6. From the strip, cut eight 4½-inch-long Supports. (Do not discard the remaining piece.) Miter both ends of each Ceiling Trim Support at a 20-degree angle, as shown in **Figure E**.

Figure C

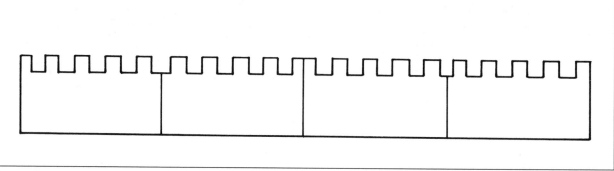

Figure D

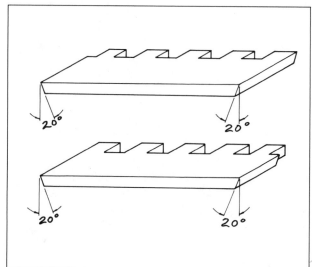

Figure E

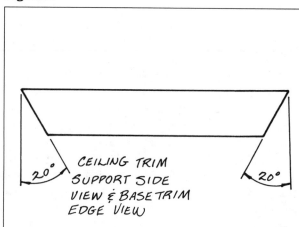

CEILING TRIM
SUPPORT SIDE
VIEW & BASE TRIM
EDGE VIEW

8. For the Base Trim, cut eight $1\frac{1}{8}$ x $4\frac{5}{8}$-inch pieces from $\frac{1}{4}$-inch plywood. Bevel both ends of each Base Trim piece at a 20-degree angle, as shown in **Figure E**.

9. Full-size patterns for the Horse Body, Foreleg, and Hind Leg are provided in **Figure F**. Trace the patterns and cut one of each piece from $\frac{1}{4}$-inch plywood. Use the cut pieces as patterns to cut three additional Horse Bodies, seven additional Forelegs, and seven additional Hind Legs from $\frac{1}{4}$-inch plywood.

10. For the Platform Trim and Cylinder Slats, rip three $\frac{1}{4}$ x $\frac{3}{4}$-inch strips, each approximately 6 feet long, from 1 x 6. From one strip, cut four $14\frac{5}{8}$-inch-long Platform Trim pieces. Bevel both ends of each Platform Trim piece at a 45-degree angle, as shown in **Figure G**. From the remaining Strips, cut twenty 7-inch-long Cylinder Slats.

11. For the Gear Support, cut a 3 x $5\frac{1}{2}$-inch piece from 1 x 6. Cut a 1 x $2\frac{1}{2}$-inch notch at both ends (**Figure H**). Drill a $\frac{3}{4}$-inch-diameter hole through the Gear Support, centered between the ends, and 2 inches from the longest edge.

12. For the Crank, cut a $1\frac{1}{2}$ x $4\frac{1}{2}$-inch piece from 1 x 6. Drill a $\frac{3}{4}$-inch-diameter hole $\frac{3}{4}$ inch from each end. Round off both ends of the Crank.

13. Cut a $4\frac{3}{4}$-inch-diameter Hub from 1 x 6. Drill a $1\frac{1}{2}$-inch-diameter hole through the center of the Hub.

14. The up-and-down action of the horses is provided by Cams, cut from 2 x 4. A full-size pattern for one Cam is provided in **Figure I**. Trace the top view pattern and cut one Cam from 2 x 4. To contour the Cam, trace the side view pattern onto one edge. Cut

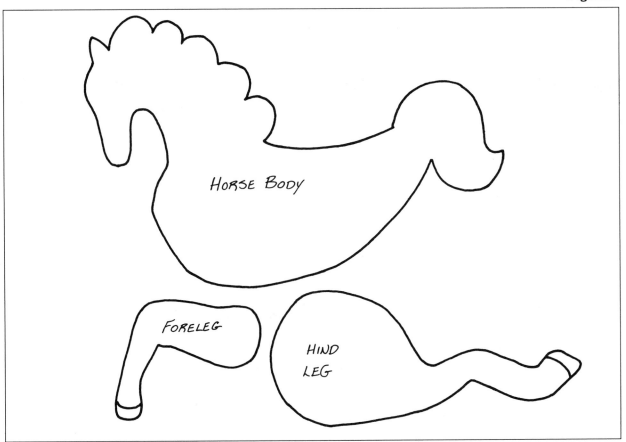

HORSE BODY

FORELEG

HIND LEG

Figure G

Figure H

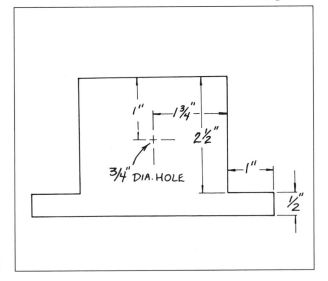

45°

45°

14 5/8"

1"

1 3/4"

2 1/2"

3/4" DIA. HOLE

1"

1/2"

Figure I

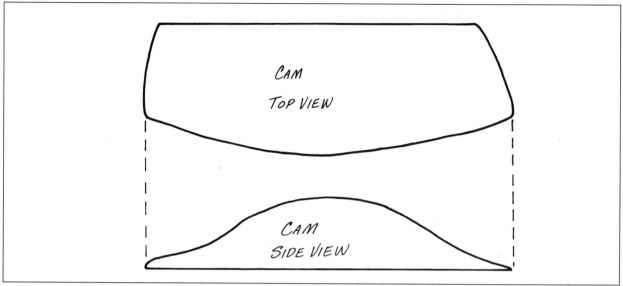

Figure J

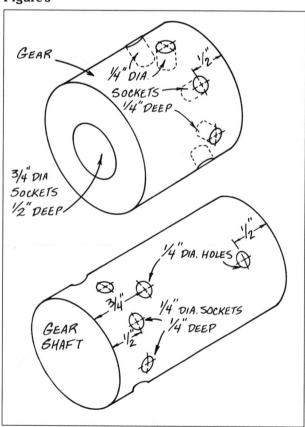

the contour at a 10-degree angle, as shown in **Figure I**. (We used a band saw, and set the table at a 10-degree angle, to make the cut.) Cut two additional Cams in the same manner.

15. Cut and label the pieces listed here from the dowel or closet rod specified.

Description	Quantity	Length	Rod
Gear	1	1¾ inches	1½-inch
Gear Shaft	1	3 inches	1½-inch
Crank Shaft	1	6 inches	¾-inch
Crank Grip	1	4 inches	¾-inch
Pivot Post	2	¾ inch	½-inch
Gear Spoke	16	1 inch	¼-inch
Horse Pole	4	9 inches	¼-inch
Flagpole	1	8 inches	¼-inch
Gear Shaft Pin	1	2 inches	¼-inch
Connecting Pin	1	3½ inches	¼-inch
Crank Shaft Pin	1	1½ inches	¼-inch
Pole Stabilizer	4	2 inches	⅛-inch

16. Drill eight evenly-spaced ¼-inch-diameter sockets, ¼ inch deep, into the curved side of the Gear, ½ inch from one end, as shown in **Figure J**. Drill a ¾-inch-diameter socket ½ inch deep into the center of the opposite end of the Gear, as shown.

THE GREAT MECHANICAL WOODEN TOY BOOK

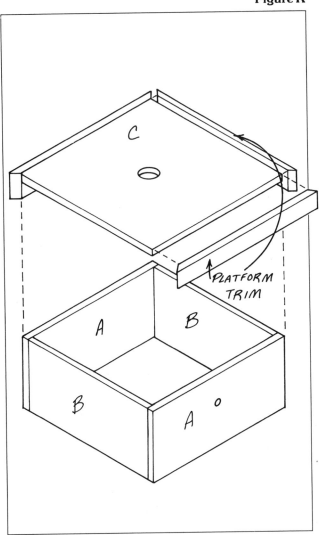

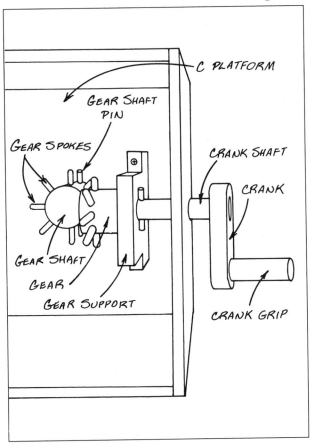

17. Drill eight sockets into the Gear Shaft ½ inch from one end, in the same manner as you did for the Gear, as shown in **Figure J**. In addition, drill a ¼-inch-diameter hole through the Gear Shaft, ¾ inch from the same drilled end. Drill a ¼-inch-diameter hole through the Gear Shaft ½ inch from the opposite end.

18. Drill a ¼-inch-diameter hole through the Crank Shaft, 4⅝ inches from one end, to accommodate the Crank Shaft Pin. So that the gears will operate smoothly, round off one end of each Gear Spoke. Also, round off one end of each Horse Pole.

Assembly

1. The platform assembly is shown in **Figure K**. Assemble a box using the A, B, and C Platform pieces, butting the edges as shown. The A pieces cover the ends of the B pieces, and the C piece covers the upper edges of the A and B pieces. The hole in the drilled A piece should be closer to the C piece, as shown. Install the Platform Trim pieces so that one edge is flush with the top of the C Platform piece.

2. The assembled gear mechanism is shown in **Figure L**. To assemble the Gear Shaft, glue a gear Spoke into each socket, so that the rounded end extends from the side of the Shaft, as shown. In addition, insert the Gear Shaft Pin through the hole just above the Spokes, leaving equal extensions on both sides. To install the Gear Shaft, insert the end opposite the Spokes up

Figure M

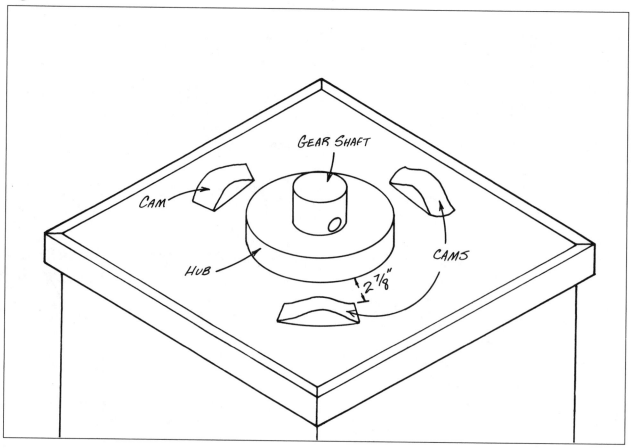

GEAR SHAFT

CAM

HUB

CAMS

2⁷⁄₈″

through the center hole in the **C** Platform, so that the Gear Shaft Pin rests against the underside of the **C** Platform, as shown.

3. The crank assembly consists of the Gear, Crank Shaft, Crank, and Crank Grip. To begin, glue a Gear Spoke into each socket in the Gear in the same manner as you did for the Gear Shaft. Insert the end of the Crank Shaft that is closer to the hole, into the socket in the Gear, and glue in place. Attach the Gear Support to the underside of the **C** Platform, 3¼ inches from the drilled **A** Platform, so that the holes are aligned, as shown in **Figure L**. Slip the Crank Shaft through the holes in the Gear Support and **A** Platform. Insert the Crank Shaft Pin into the hole in the Crank Shaft and glue in place. Slip the Crank over the end of the Crank Shaft that extends from the side of the platform, and

glue in place. Insert one end of the Crank Grip into the remaining hole in the Crank and glue in place.

4. Install each of the three Cams on the top of the platform, as shown in **Figure M**. Rub beeswax on the surface of each Cam. Slip the Hub over the Gear Shaft, as shown, and glue it to the top of the platform, being careful not to glue the Hub to the Shaft.

5. Assemble the floor as shown in **Figure N**. Attach the Floor Trim pieces to the Floor so that one edge of the trim is flush with the top of the Floor. Glue a Pivot Post into each ½-inch-diameter hole in the Floor so that one end of each Post is flush with the underside of the Floor and the holes are aligned as shown.

6. To install the floor, slip it over the Gear Shaft with the Floor Trim extending toward the platform, and align the holes in the Gear Shaft and the Pivot Posts,

THE GREAT MECHANICAL WOODEN TOY BOOK

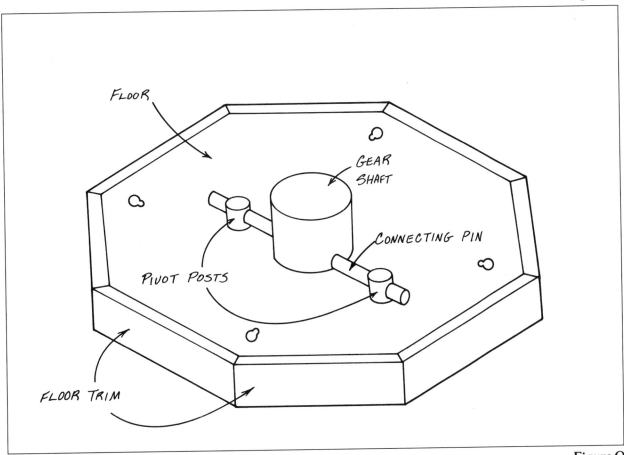

FLOOR

GEAR SHAFT

CONNECTING PIN

PIVOT POSTS

FLOOR TRIM

as shown in **Figure N**. Insert the Connecting Pin through the holes in the Pivot Posts and Gear Shaft to secure the floor to the gear mechanism.

7. The assembled cylinder is shown in **Figure O**. Glue and nail the Cylinder Slats to the outer curved edges of the two Rings to create the cylinder. The ends of the Cylinder Slats should be flush with the outer side of the Ring at each end. You may have to cut the last Slat lengthwise to make it fit.

8. Attach the Ceiling Trim Supports to one side of the Ceiling, so that the outer edge of each Support is flush with the edge of the Ceiling, as shown in **Figure P**. Attach the Ceiling Trim pieces so that the lower edges are flush with the underside of the Ceiling, as shown. Glue the Flagpole into the center hole in the Ceiling.

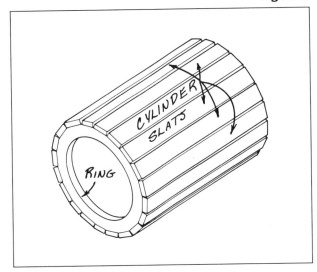

CYLINDER SLATS

RING

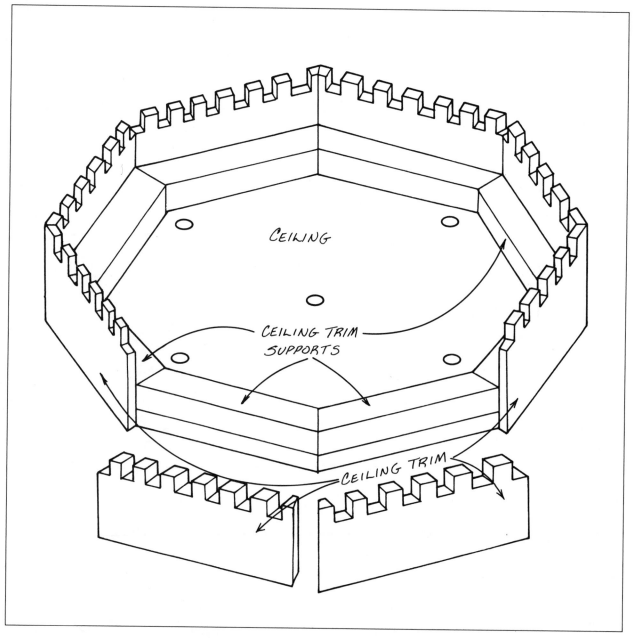

CEILING

CEILING TRIM
SUPPORTS

CEILING TRIM

9. Center the cylinder on the underside of the Ceiling and secure with glue and screws inserted through the Ceiling into the Ring.

10. Assemble one horse using glue and brads, as shown in **Figure Q**. Assemble three additional Horses in the same manner. Glue each horse to a Horse Pole, approximately 3 inches from the rounded end of the Pole. Glue a Pole Stabilizer to each Horse Pole, on the side opposite the horse, as shown.

11. To install the horses, insert the lower rounded

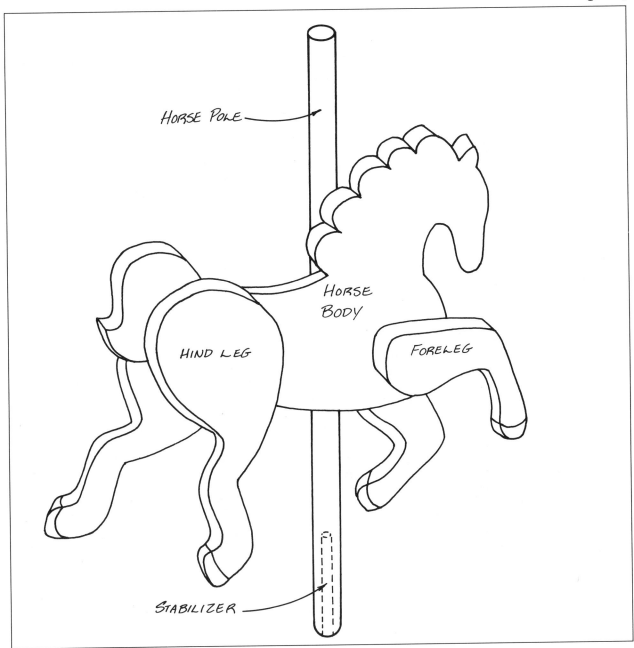

HORSE POLE

HORSE BODY

HIND LEG

FORELEG

STABILIZER

end of each Horse Pole into a hole in the Floor, as shown in **Figure R**. Rotate the Horse Pole until the Pole Stabilizer slips down into the smaller hole adjacent to each horse pole hole.

12. To install the ceiling and cylinder assembly, place it down over the Floor so that the upper end of each Horse Pole slides into a hole in the Ceiling, as shown in **Figure R**. Glue the assembly to the Floor.

Figure R

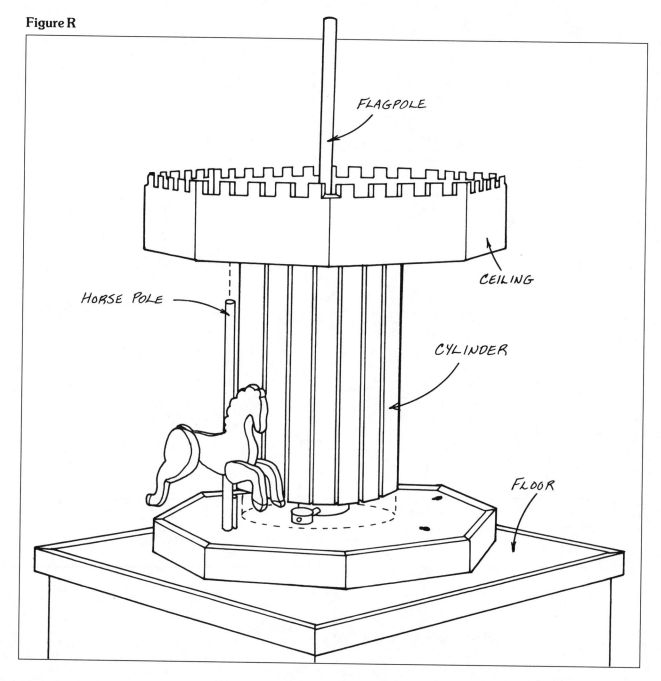

FLAGPOLE

CEILING

HORSE POLE

CYLINDER

FLOOR

Adding the Canopy

1. A full-size pattern for the Canopy is provided in **Figure S**. Trace the pattern and cut seven Canopy pieces from canvas.

2. To assemble the canopy, place two Canopy pieces right sides together and stitch a ½-inch-wide seam along one long edge, as shown in **Figure T**. Open out the two pieces and place them right side up on a flat sur-

THE GREAT MECHANICAL WOODEN TOY BOOK

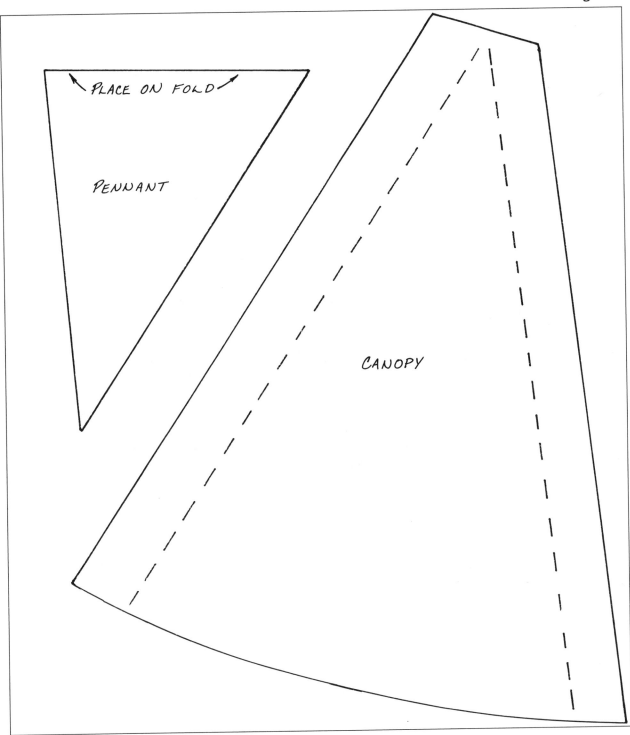

PLACE ON FOLD

PENNANT

CANOPY

SPINNING CAROUSEL

Figure T

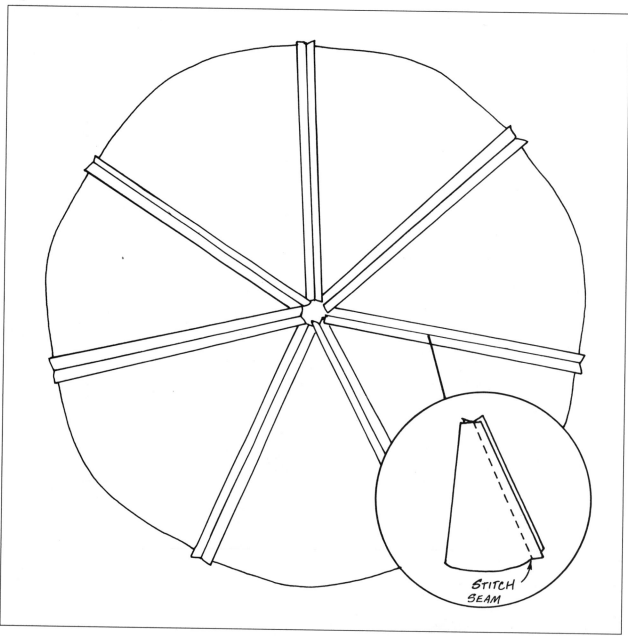

STITCH
SEAM

face. Place another piece right side down on top. Stitch the seam along one long edge. Continue adding pieces in this manner until you have assembled all the pieces into a circle, as shown.

3. Slip the center hole of the assembled canopy over the Flagpole, and glue the canopy to the Flagpole 2¼ inches from the top, as shown in **Figure U**. Spread the canopy out over the top of the carousel, and glue the outer edge to the Ceiling Supports.

4. A full-size pattern for the Pennant is provided in

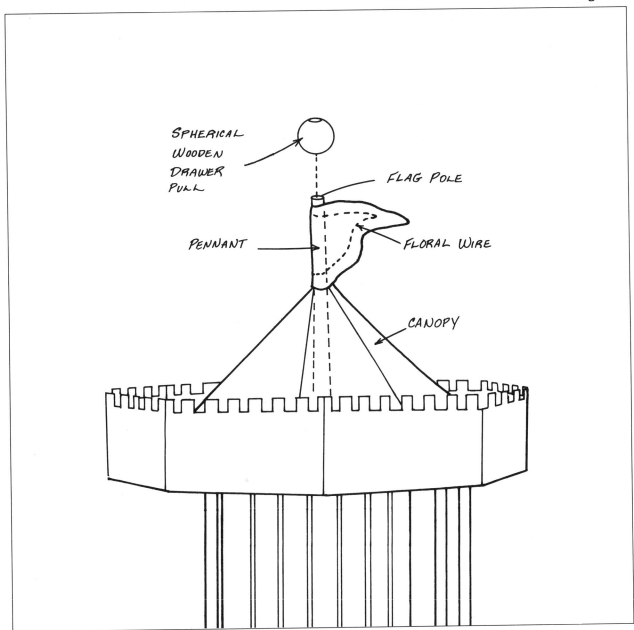

SPHERICAL
WOODEN
DRAWER
PULL

FLAG POLE

PENNANT

FLORAL WIRE

CANOPY

Figure S. Trace the pattern and cut one Pennant from felt, being sure to place one edge of the pattern on a fold, as indicated.

5. To install the Pennant, attach the floral wire to the Flagpole as shown in **Figure U**. Spread glue on one side of the Pennant, and fold it around the Flagpole and wire, as shown, pressing the glued sides together.

6. Drill a ¼-inch-diameter socket into the spherical wooden drawer pull (if it doesn't already have one). Glue the drawer pull to the top of the Flagpole.

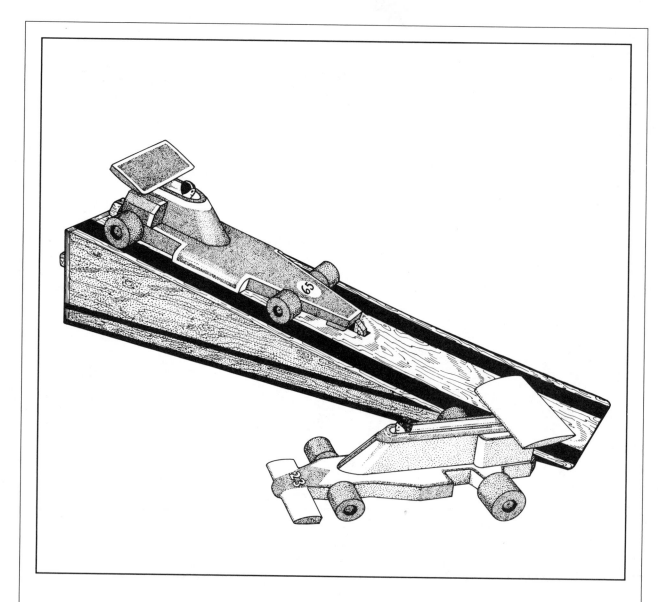

Catapult Cars

These jack-rabbit dragsters literally zoom off the ramp, powered by a rubber-band catapult. Youngsters can recreate the thrill of the speedway for hours of fun, in competition with each other or with the stopwatch. Overall dimensions of the single-car ramp are approximately 6 x 9 x 30 inches.

Figure A

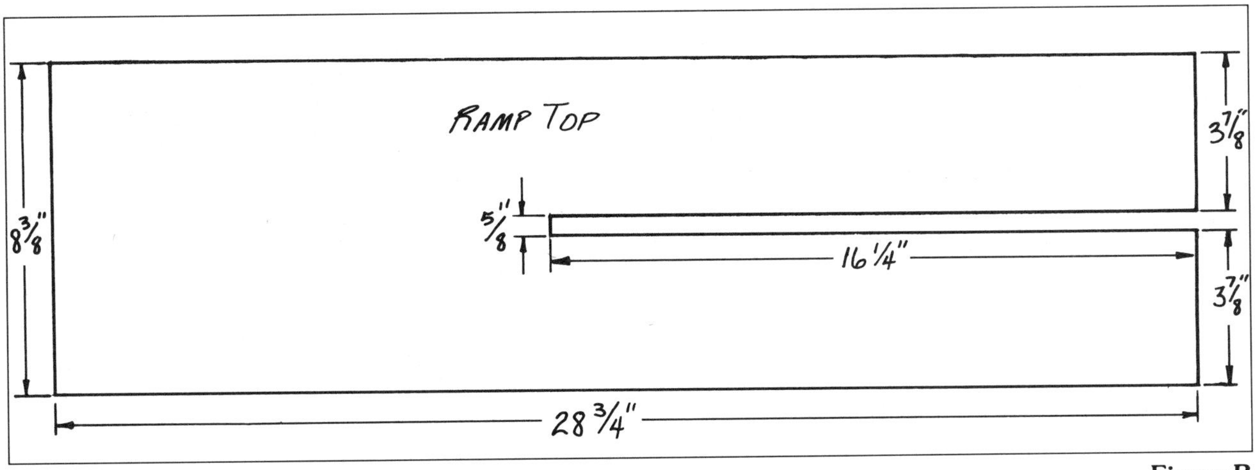
RAMP TOP
5/8"
16 1/4"
3 7/8"
3 7/8"
8 3/8"
28 3/4"

Figure B

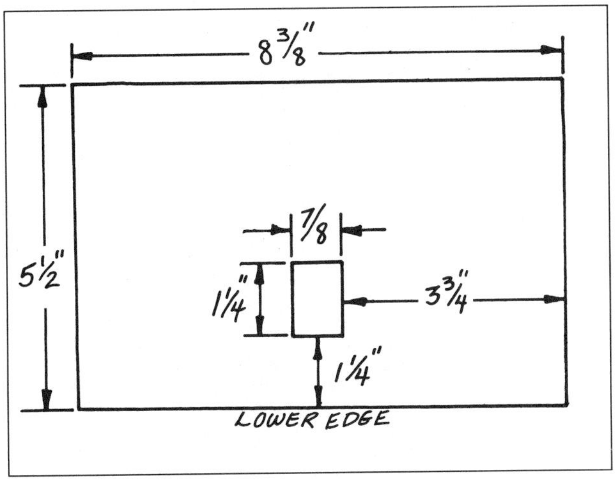
8 3/8"
7/8
5 1/2"
1 1/4"
3 3/4"
1 1/4"
LOWER EDGE

Materials

Note: We have listed sufficient materials to build one single-car ramp and two different racers. You may wish to build an additional ramp so that two cars can be catapulted at the same time. Once you have the hang of how the cars are put together, you also may wish to design and build additional cars.

10 x 30-inch piece of 1/8-inch veneer-core plywood, finished on both sides

6 x 10-inch piece of 1/2-inch veneer-core plywood, finished on both sides

7 linear feet of pine 1 x 6

2 linear feet of pine 2 x 2

Wooden dowel or closet rod: 3-foot length of 1/4-inch-diameter; 2-inch length of 1/2-inch-diameter; 2-inch length of 7/8-inch-diameter; 8-inch length of 1 1/4-inch-diameter; 8-inch length of 1 3/4-inch-diameter

Dowel people: One 3/4 inch in diameter, and one 5/8 inch in diameter (see Tips & Techniques)

18 gauge wire brads, 3/4 inch long; and 3d finishing nails

Two screwhooks, each about 1 inch long with a 3/8-inch-diameter hook; and one larger screwhook, about 1 1/2 inches long with a 3/4-inch-diameter hook

Four heavy-duty rubber bands, each approximately 3 inches long

Carpenter's wood glue; beeswax; wood stain or vegetable oil; and non-toxic paints in your choice of colors (We used red, yellow, and black.)

Cutting the Plywood

1. For the Ramp Top, cut an 8 3/4 x 28 3/4-inch rectangle from 1/8-inch plywood. Cut a 5/8 x 16 1/4-inch groove into one end of the Ramp Top, centered between the edges, as shown in **Figure A**.

2. For the Ramp Back, cut a 5 1/2 x 8 3/4-inch rectangle from 1/2-inch plywood. Cut a 7/8 x 1 1/4-inch mortise through the Ramp Back, 1 1/4 inches from one edge (this will be the lower edge) and centered between the ends, as shown in **Figure B**. (We cheated a bit by cutting straight upward from the lower edge and then along the outlines of the mortise. This left a narrow slit from the lower edge up to the mortise, but because there will be

Figure C

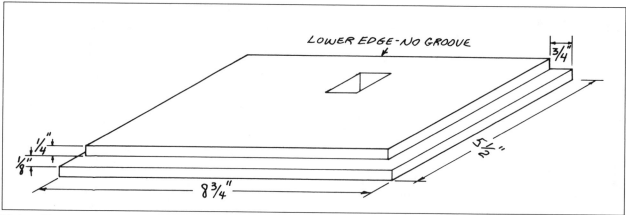

LOWER EDGE-NO GROOVE

3/4"

1/4"

1/8"

5½"

8¾"

Figure D

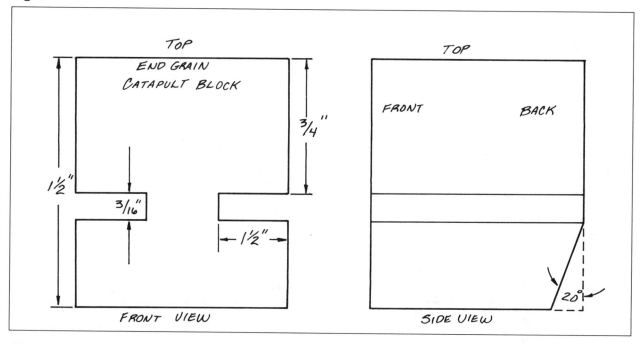

TOP

END GRAIN
CATAPULT BLOCK

3/4"

1½"

3/16"

1½"

FRONT VIEW

TOP

FRONT   BACK

20°

SIDE VIEW

no stress on the Ramp Back, it really doesn't matter. This approach is much easier than drilling through the piece and then cutting the mortise.)

3. The Ramp Back must also be grooved to accommodate the Ramp Sides and Top. Cut a ¼ x ¾-inch groove along each end of the Ramp Back, and cut a ¼ x ⅛-inch groove along the upper edge, as shown in **Figure C**. All grooves should be cut along the same side of the piece, as shown.

Cutting the 2 x 2

1. Cut a 1½-inch length of 2 x 2 for the Catapult Block. The surfaces that present end grain will be the front and back of the Block. Cut a 3/16 x ½-inch groove along each side of the Block from front to back, as shown in the front view drawing, **Figure D**. Drill a shallow pilot socket into the front of the Block, ¼ inch below and centered between the grooves, using a bit

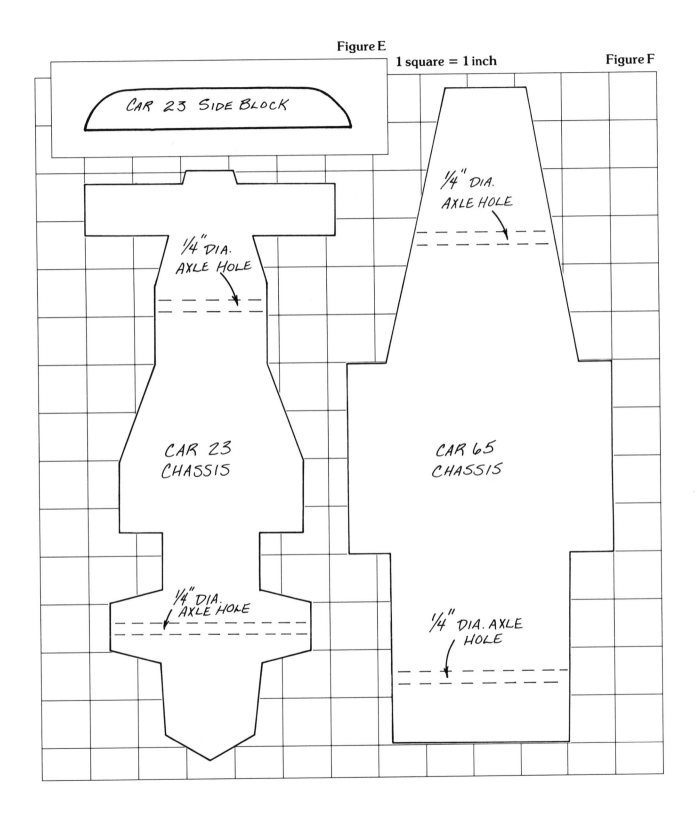

1 square = 1 inch

Figure F

CAR 23 SIDE BLOCK

¼" DIA. AXLE HOLE

¼" DIA. AXLE HOLE

CAR 23 CHASSIS

CAR 65 CHASSIS

¼" DIA. AXLE HOLE

¼" DIA. AXLE HOLE

Figure G

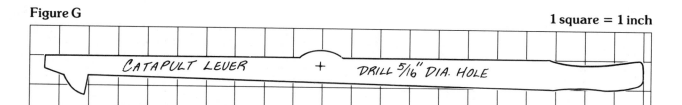

CATAPULT LEVER   +   DRILL 5/16" DIA. HOLE

Figure H

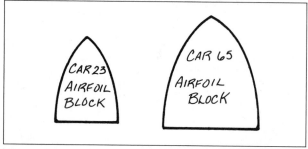

CAR 23 AIRFOIL BLOCK

CAR 65 AIRFOIL BLOCK

that is slightly smaller in diameter than the threaded shank of the larger screwhook. Bevel the back of the Block below the grooves at a 20-degree angle, as shown in the side view drawing, **Figure D**.

2. Cut a 9½-inch length of 2 x 2 for the Car 23 Body. (We gave our cars racing numbers: Car 23 and Car 65.) Rip the Body piece to a width of 1⅛ inches; it should now measure 1⅛ x 1½ x 9½ inches. The contours will be cut later.

Figure I

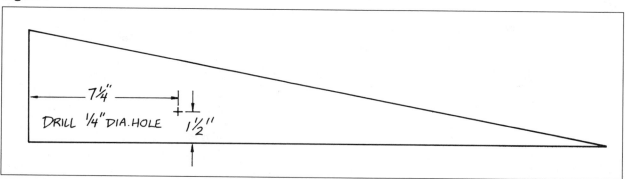

7¼"

DRILL ¼" DIA. HOLE   1½"

Figure J

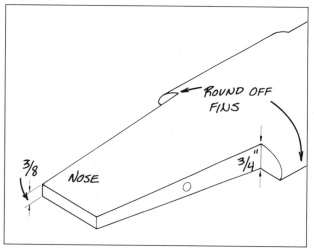

ROUND OFF FINS

3/8   NOSE   3/4"

Figure K

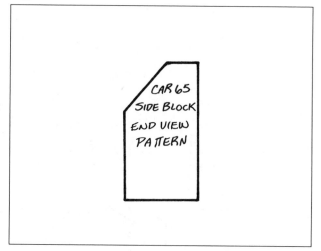

CAR 65 SIDE BLOCK END VIEW PATTERN

3. A full-size pattern for the Car 23 Side Block is provided in **Figure E**. Trace the pattern and cut two Car 23 Side Blocks from the remaining pine 2 x 2.

Cutting the 1 x 6

1. Scale drawings for the Catapult Lever, Car 23 Chassis, and Car 65 Chassis are provided in **Figures F** and **G**. Enlarge the drawings to make full-size patterns. For the Airfoil Blocks, trace the full-size patterns provided in **Figure H**. Cut the pieces listed in this step from 1 x 6 pine. Where no dimensions are listed, use the full-size pattern that you traced or enlarged.

Part	Quantity	Dimensions
Ramp Side	1	5½ x 28 inches
Catapult Lever	1	Figure F
Lever Support	1	½ x 6⅞ inches
Car 23 Chassis	1	Figure F
Car 65 Chassis	1	Figure F
Car 65 Body	2	2 x 6¼ inches
Car 65 Side Block	2	1¾ x 2 inches
Car 23 Airfoil Block	1	Figure G
Car 65 Airfoil Block	1	Figure G

2. Some of the pieces that you cut from 1 x 6 must be modified. Cut diagonally across the Ramp Side piece to create two triangular Ramp Sides like the one shown in **Figure I**. Temporarily nail the two Ramp Sides together, using small finishing nails, and drill a ¼-inch-diameter hole through both, 7¼ inches from the

back end and 1½ inches from the lower edge, as shown. Remove the holding nails.

3. Drill a hole ⁵⁄₁₆ inch in diameter through the Catapult Lever, where indicated on the scale drawing (**Figure G**). Sand the edges smooth at the handle end of the Lever, and lightly sand the rest of the Lever.

4. Drill two ¼-inch-diameter axle holes through each Car Chassis piece from edge to edge, where indicated by dotted lines on the scale drawings (**Figure F**). For the Car 65 Chassis, choose one side as the top and bevel the top side of the nose portion, so that the front end is only ⅜ inch thick, as shown in **Figure J**. Round off the top edge of each fin, as shown. For the Car 23 Chassis, bevel the top side of the nose portion, between the front axle hole and the nose end, in the same manner as you did the Car 65 Chassis. Completely round off the nose end of the Car 23 Chassis.

5. The Car 65 Side Blocks also must be modified. A full-size pattern is provided in **Figure K**. Trace the pattern and place your traced pattern against one end of one Car 65 Side Block. Trim the piece to match the pattern. Repeat these procedures to trim the second Car 65 Side Block. Choose one end of each piece as the front end, and bevel the top front edge at a slight angle. Bevel the two outer front edges as well, but do not bevel the long inner edge or the lower edge. When you bevel the second Block, be sure you have it turned the right way; the finished pieces should be mirror images of each other, as shown in the diagram of the assembled car, **Figure T**.

6. Each of the Airfoil Blocks must be modified.

Figure L

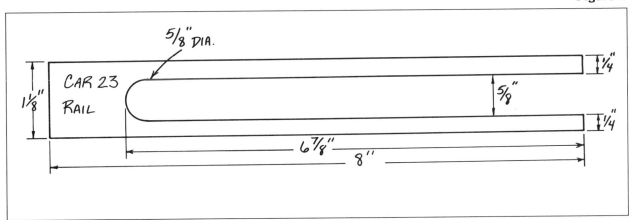

Figure M

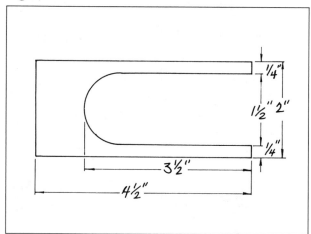

Choose one side of the Car 65 Airfoil Block as the top, and bevel the top at a 12-degree angle toward the pointed front end. Bevel the top of the Car 23 Airfoil Block at a 10-degree angle toward the front end.

7. Stack and glue together the two Car 65 Body pieces, so that you have a single piece 2 x 6¼ inches, 1½ inches thick. Clamp the assembly and allow it to dry while you finish cutting the remaining pieces. It will be shaped later.

8. The remaining pieces are cut from 1 x 6 pine that has been sliced to ¼- or ⅜-inch thick. Slice a sufficient amount of 1 x 6 stock to the required thicknesses, and cut the pieces listed in this step.

Part	Quantity	Dimensions
Airfoil	2	¼ x 2½ x 6 inches
Nose Block	1	¼ x ¾ x 2⅛ inches
Car 23 Rail	1	⅜ x 1⅛ x 8 inches
Car 65 Rail	1	⅜ x 2 x 4½ inches

9. The Car 23 Rail piece must be modified as shown in **Figure L**. Cut a ⅝ x 6⅞-inch groove into one end of the piece, as shown. The inner end of the groove should be rounded.

Figure N

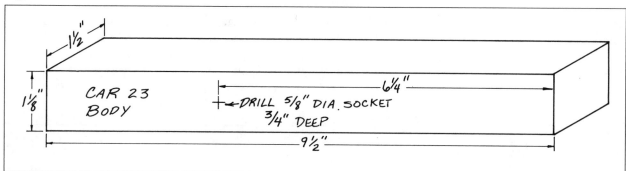

Figure O

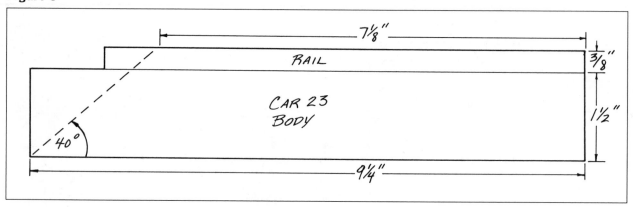

Figure P

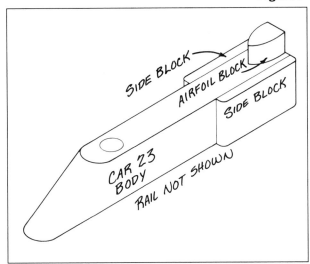

SIDE BLOCK
AIRFOIL BLOCK
SIDE BLOCK
CAR 23 BODY
RAIL NOT SHOWN

Figure Q

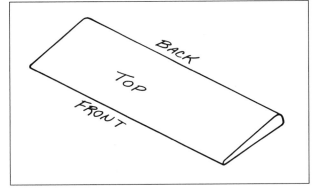

BACK
TOP
FRONT

10. The Car 65 Rail piece must be modified as shown in **Figure M**. Cut a 1½ x 3½-inch groove into one end. The inner end of the groove should be rounded.

Figure R

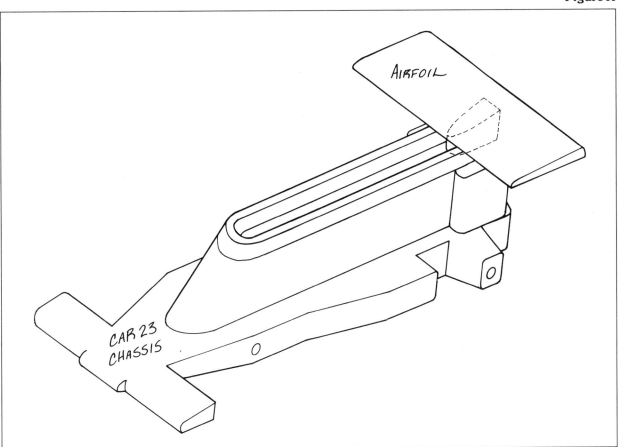

AIRFOIL
CAR 23 CHASSIS

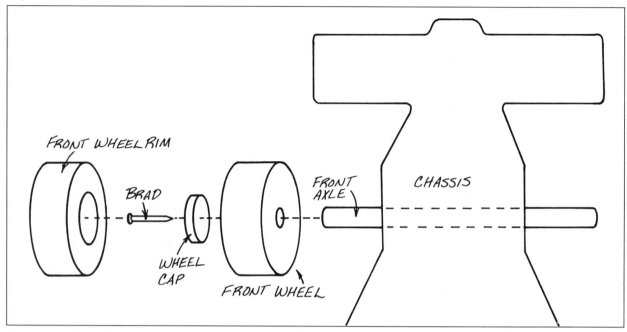

FRONT WHEEL RIM

BRAD

WHEEL CAP

FRONT WHEEL

FRONT AXLE

CHASSIS

Assembling Car 23

The body of each car consists of Rail, Body, and Side Block pieces. An Airfoil Block supports the contoured Airfoil at an angle at the back of the car. The body contains a socket that accommodates a dowel-person driver. The assembled body is glued to the Chassis, and axles and wheels are installed on the Chassis. Car 23 is shown completely assembled, minus the wheels and driver, in **Figure R**.

1. You already have cut the Car 23 Body piece, which must be drilled to accommodate the driver. Drill a ⅝-inch-diameter socket, ¾ inch deep, into one of the 1⅛-inch-wide edges, as shown in **Figure N**. The socket should be placed 6¼ inches from one end, and centered between the wider edges, as shown.

2. Glue the contoured Car 23 Rail piece to the drilled edge of the Body piece. The grooved end of the Rail should be flush with the end of the Body piece that is farthest from the socket, and all side edges should be even. When the glue has dried, measure along the Rail 7⅛ inches from the grooved end, and mark this point. Bevel the front end of the assembly from the marked

point on the Rail to the lower front end of the Body, as shown in **Figure O**; this should be an angle of about 40 degrees. Use a sander or band saw to round off the beveled front end, as shown in **Figure P**.

3. Glue a Car 23 Side Block to each side of the assembled body as shown in **Figure P**. The two Blocks should be flush with the back end and lower surface of the Body piece.

4. Glue the Car 23 Airfoil Block to the upper edge of the Body piece between the rails, as shown in **Figure P**. The pointed end of the Block should face the front of the car body, and the tallest (back) edge should be flush with the back end of the body.

5. We used a sander to bevel and shape one of the Airfoil pieces as shown in **Figure Q**. As you can see, the upper surface of the piece is beveled toward the front, so that the long front edge is quite thin. The upper back edge is rounded off. Shape one of the Airfoil pieces, and glue it to the Airfoil Block on Car 23 as shown in **Figure R**. The back edge of the Airfoil should extend about ⅝ inch beyond the back end of the Block. Glue the body assembly to the Car 23 Chassis piece, as shown. Sand all exposed edges and surfaces.

6. Each wheel consists of two short lengths of closet rod, drilled and glued together. A separate Wheel Cap serves to hold the wheel on the axle. To make one front wheel, cut two ¾-inch lengths of 1¼-inch closet rod. Drill a ¼-inch-diameter axle hole through the center of one, and label this piece as the Front Wheel. Drill a ½-inch-diameter hole through the center of the other, and label this piece as the Front Wheel Rim. Cut a ¼-inch length of ½-inch dowel rod for the Wheel Cap. Cut, drill, and label identical pieces for the second front wheel. Sand all of the pieces carefully, including the edges of the holes. Cut a 4¼-inch length of ¼-inch dowel rod for the Front Axle.

7. The front wheel assembly is shown in **Figure S**. Insert the axle through the front axle hole in the chassis, leaving equal extensions on each side. Glue the axle in place and rub beeswax on the extending ends. Install a Front Wheel over one end of the axle, but do not use glue. Glue a Wheel Cap to the end of the axle, centering it precisely, and drive a brad through the center of the Wheel Cap into the center of the axle end. Glue a Front Wheel Rim to the Front Wheel, being careful not to allow the glue to seep out inside the assembly; you don't want to glue the Rim to the Wheel Cap. Assemble the second front wheel on the other end of the axle in the same manner.

8. The rear wheels are assembled in the same manner as the front wheels, but they are larger. For one rear wheel, cut two ¾-inch lengths of 1½-inch-diameter closet rod. Drill a ¼-inch-diameter axle hole through the center of one, and label it as the Rear Wheel. Drill a ⅞-inch-diameter hole through the center of the other, and label it as the Rear Wheel Rim. Cut a ¼-inch length of ⅞-inch-diameter dowel rod for the Wheel Cap. Cut, drill, and label identical pieces for the second rear wheel, and sand all pieces carefully. Cut a 6⅛-inch length of ¼-inch dowel for the Rear Axle.

9. Follow the procedures described in step 7 to install the Rear Axle and rear wheels.

10. Paint only the head portion of the ⅝-inch-diameter dowel person. We used black paint to create small eye dots, a mustache, and a racing helmet. When the black paint had dried, we added a small red mouth, pink cheek spots, a pink nose dot, and a red stripe along the center of the helmet. Insert the dowel person into the socket in the top of the car body to test for height. We trimmed off the bottom of the dowel person so that the head extends only about ⅝ inch above the upper edges of the car rails. You can glue the driver into the socket, or leave it unglued so the kids can remove and lose it.

11. Paint the car in your choice of colors, being careful not to allow any paint to drip into the inner workings of the wheels. We painted the car yellow all over, and allowed the yellow to dry. We then added red details: the upper edges and outer surfaces of the rails, a stripe down the front of the body, thin outlines along the upper edges of the side blocks and chassis, and a large solid triangle on the nose portion of the chassis. We painted the wheels black, and added a yellow "23" to the red portion of the nose.

Assembling Car 65

1. The second car is assembled in much the same manner as the first one. You already have cut and glued together the two Car 65 Body pieces to create a single Body. The Body must be drilled to accommodate the driver. Drill a ¾-inch-diameter socket ¾ inch deep into one wide side of the Body, 2¾ inches from one end and centered between the edges.

2. Glue the contoured Car 65 Rail piece to the drilled side of the Body. The grooved end of the Rail should be flush with the end of the Body that is closest to the socket, and all side edges should be even. When the glue has dried, measure along the Rail piece 3⅞ inches from the grooved end, and mark this point. Bevel the front end of the assembly from the marked point on the Rail to the lower front end of the Body, as you did for the first car; this should be an angle of about 35 degrees. Use a sander or a band saw to round off the beveled front end.

3. Glue a Car 65 Side Block to each side of the assembled body as shown in **Figure T**. The beveled edges of each Block should face front, and the back of each Block should be flush with the back end of the body. The lower edges of the Blocks should be flush with the bottom of the body. Glue the Car 65 Airfoil Block to the body, between the rails as shown. Glue the assembled body to the Car 65 Chassis, with all back ends flush.

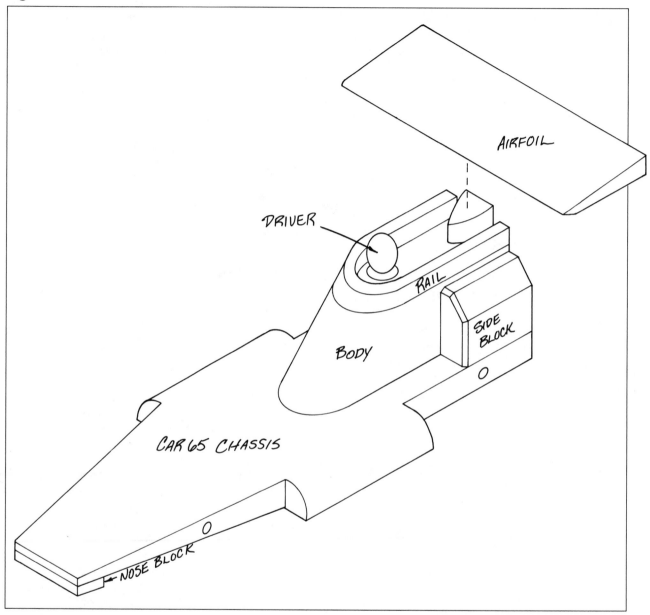

4. Bevel and shape the remaining Airfoil piece as you did for Car 23. For Car 65, we turned the Airfoil so that the beveled side faces downward. Glue the Airfoil to the Airfoil Block, as shown in **Figure T**. The back edge of the Airfoil should extend about ¾ inch beyond the back end of the Block. Glue the Nose Block piece to the underside of the Chassis, flush with the front end. Sand all exposed edges and surfaces of the car.

5. The wheels for Car 65 are identical to those for Car 23. Refer back to steps 6 through 9 in the last section ("Assembling Car 23"), and cut the same pieces for Car 65 wheels. The axles are slightly different in size:

For Car 65, cut a 4⅞-inch length of ¼-inch dowel for the Front Axle, and a 5⅝-inch length for the Rear Axle. Install the axles and assemble the wheels as you did for Car 23.

6. Paint the head portion of the ¾-inch-diameter dowel person, trim it to the desired length, and install it in the driver socket. Paint the car in your choice of colors. We painted the entire car red, and added yellow outline details. We painted a yellow circle on the nose portion of the car, and added a red "65." The wheels are black.

Assembling the Ramp

1. Insert the larger screwhook into the pilot socket that you drilled into the Catapult Block. Give it a final twist so that the opening in the hook faces the top of the Block. Slip the Block into the groove in the Ramp Top piece, hook end first.

2. Assemble the basic ramp structure as shown in **Figure U**. The back ends of the two Ramp Sides fit into the grooves that were cut along the ends of the Ramp Back piece, and the back end of the Ramp Top fits into the groove that was cut along the upper edge of the Back piece. The Ramp Top covers the upper edges of the Ramp Sides.

3. The Lever Support is installed inside the ramp as shown in **Figure V**. Turn the ramp upside down and place the Lever Support across the underside of the Ramp Top, 2½ inches from the front end of the groove. The Support should be turned so that one wide side is flat against the Ramp Top. Before you attach the Support, be sure that the Catapult Block is behind the Support, not between the Support and the front of the groove. Glue the Support to the Ramp Sides and Top, and secure it by driving nails through the Sides into the ends of the Support. Drill pilot holes and insert a small screwhook into the Lever Support ⅝ inch from each end, as shown in **Figure V**. Turn each hook so that the opening faces the adjacent Ramp Side.

4. Leave the ramp turned upside down as you install the lever mechanism. Insert the front end of the Lever (the end closest to the little triangular extension) through the mortise in the Ramp Back, from the outside inward. Be sure that the Lever is turned so that the edge with the triangular extension faces the underside of the Ramp Top. Push the Lever through the mortise until the front end is about even with the front of the groove in the Ramp Top. Allow the front end of the Lever to drop downward so that the triangular extension falls into the Ramp Top groove, in front of the Lever Support. The hole that was drilled through the Lever should be aligned with the holes in the Ramp Sides.

5. Cut an 8½-inch length of ¼-inch dowel rod and insert it through the hole in one Ramp Side, from the outside inward. Guide it through the hole in the Lever, and into the hole in the opposite Ramp Side. Adjust the dowel so that the ends are flush with the outer surfaces of the Ramp Sides. It need not be glued in place; if you wish to do so, glue it to the Ramp Sides but not to the Lever, because the Lever must pivot on it.

6. Anchor one end of a rubber band around the screwhook at one end of the Lever Support. Stretch the rubber band over the Lever and anchor the other end around the screwhook at the opposite end of the Lever Support (**Figure V**). Install a second rubber band in the same manner. Install a third rubber band between the screwhook at one end of the Lever Support, and the larger screwhook at the front of the Catapult Block. Install a fourth rubber band between the screwhook at the opposite end of the Lever Support, and the screwhook at the front of the Catapult Block.

7. We sanded and stained all outer surfaces of the ramp, the handle end of the Lever, and the portion of the Catapult Block that extends above the Ramp Top. When the stain had dried, we painted a wide black stripe along each edge of the Ramp Top, and two narrower stripes along each Ramp Side.

Catapulting the Cars

To make this contraption work, pull back on the catapult block so that it slides up the groove toward the back of the ramp, and hold it there. Place one of the cars on the ramp, with the nose flush against the triangular portion of the lever that extends up through the groove. Allow the block to slide forward so that it rests against the back of the car. At the sound of the starting gun, pull upward on the handle end of the lever. This action will lower the front end of the lever, releasing the car and allowing the rubber bands attached to the catapult block to contract.

Figure U

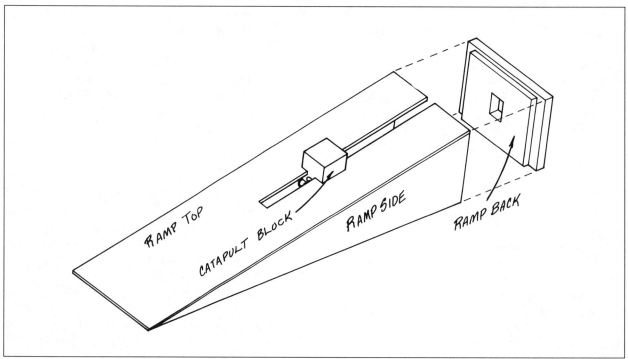

RAMP TOP

CATAPULT BLOCK

RAMP SIDE

RAMP BACK

Figure V

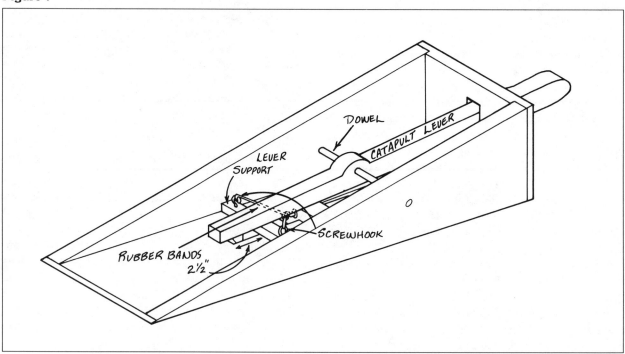

DOWEL

CATAPULT LEVER

LEVER SUPPORT

SCREWHOOK

RUBBER BANDS 2½"

THE GREAT MECHANICAL WOODEN TOY BOOK

About the Family...

The Family Workshop, a one-of-a-kind creative idea company, is located in Bixby, Oklahoma. The company specializes in the field of how-to, with subjects ranging from fabric crafts and woodworking to home improvement, photography, and computers.

The Family Workshop originated, quite literally, on the Baldwins' front porch. Ed and Stevie, long-time hobbyists and experts in the do-it-yourself field, began writing a newspaper column called "Makin' Things." Since 1977, the family has grown to include other craftspersons, woodworkers, artists, and editors, who have helped provide the public with do-it-yourself tips, pointers, and projects through television programs, syndicated columns, quarterly newsletters, and a series of books for a number of major publishing houses.

Ed and Stevie, nationally known and respected how-to newspaper columnists, appeared in over 100 segments of a TV series that provided viewers time- and money-saving ideas for making things at home.

This energetic couple also has done a number of product promotions for major companies in the do-it-yourself field, as well as appearing in various TV commercials. They have been featured in training films and demonstrations for several different organizations.

Since the birth of the company, the Baldwins and their staff have authored and produced more than a dozen how-to books. These publications include subjects such as family computers, furniture building, and making projects from fabric scraps. Impressively, nine of the books have been either main, featured alternate, or alternate selections for either the Better Homes & Gardens or Popular Science book clubs.

The Family Workshop currently produces three syndicated weekly newspaper columns. The original craft-oriented column, "Makin' Things," was first written and produced in 1975. Since that time, Ed and Stevie and their staff have created two additional columns: "The Woodwright," and "Kid's Stuff." The three columns appear weekly in publications with a combined readership of over 26 million. "Classified Crafts," their most recent newspaper service, was started in 1983. The Family Workshop's newspaper features run in more than 500 daily and weekly newspapers across the country, with more than 750 appearances per week.